Dying a

CW00347280

SERIES EDITOR
June Clark BA MPhil SRN HVCert

In the Same Series

TOPICS IN COMMUNITY HEALTH

Dying at Home

HARRIET COPPERMAN SRN SCM NDN Cert

Nursing Sister, Symptom Control/Support Team,
Royal Free Hospital, London; previously a Founder
Member and First Nursing Director,
The Macmillan Service, St. Joseph's
Hospice, London

Foreword by

DAME CICELY SAUNDERS DBE FRCP

Medical Director, St Christopher's Hospice,
Sydenham, London; Hon. Consultant,
St Joseph's Hospice, Hackney, London

An HM + M Nursing Publication

JOHN WILEY & SONS

Chichester · New York · Brisbane · Toronto · Singapore

HM + M is an imprint of John Wiley & Sons Ltd

Reprinted March 1986
Reprinted September 1988

Library of Congress Cataloging in Publication Data:

Copperman, Harriet.
  Dying at home.

  (Topics in community health) (An HM + M nursing
publication)
  Bibliography: p.
  Includes index.
  1. Home nursing. 2. Terminal care. 3. Terminal
care — Psychological aspects. 4. Cancer — Psychological
aspects. 5. Death — Psychological aspects. I. Title.
II. Series: Topics in community health (John Wiley
& Sons) III. Series: HM + M nursing publication.
[DNLM: 1. Terminal care — Nursing texts. 2. Home care
services — Nursing texts. WY 152 C785d]

RT61.C67 1983   649.8   83-9903
ISBN 0 471 26278 1 (U.S.)

British Cataloguing in Publication Data:

Copperman, Harriet
  Dying at home. — (Topics in community health). —
(An HM & M nursing publication)
  1. Terminal care   2. Death
  I. Title   II. Series
  362.1   R726.8

  ISBN 0 471 26278 1

Printed and bound in Great Britain

Contents

Contents

Foreword

This valuable book begins aptly with a quotation from Florence Nightingale, "The most important practical lesson that can be given to nurses is to teach them what to observe—how to observe". In the chapters that follow we are shown how a nurse, observing compassionately and acutely, has learned and developed the broad aims and the details of home care for dying patients. Members of all disciplines and many families will find help and encouragement in its practical wisdom. Good nursing is the cornerstone of home care at the end of a patient's life and this in turn depends on imaginative and effective symptom control, together with some knowledge of how to ease family distress. Workers in different disciplines combine into a team as they understand each other's roles more fully and anyone reading this book will learn better not only what nurses have to offer but also how to share effectively in joint work and planning.

It has been said that man is adapted to being cared for because of his profound dependence at birth. It could also be said that we are equally adapted to caring. From her 'gut assessment' of a home situation on to the finer details of making someone comfortable, Harriet Copperman has described her special area of courteous caring. At the same time, however, she has never lost sight of not only the family members' need to fulfil the end of a life together but also how to maintain the essential independence of the person being cared for. All of us in this field discover repeatedly how some people use their last weeks or days to complete or affirm the deepest meaning of their lives. The way to making this possible is made up of many simple things, for the nurse to do herself or, more often, for the home carer to be taught and encouraged to do.

Some of the activity and support described here may seem elementary but as Harriet Copperman points out, "from time to time we all need to reflect on our basic approaches to the patients in order to perceive the need to modify our practice''. We can all appreciate her attention to detail, the description of how 'an enthusiastic nurse with a pair of good nail clippers can make a patient feel thoroughly pampered' or how the simple act of turning back on the doorstep can encourage the last, all-important question.

She emphasizes the importance of helping the patient and carer to talk together of the illness and its outcome. ''An enormous feeling of weight and burden is lifted from everyone when a husband and wife begin to communicate freely and support each other.'' Even the less good marriages can move into the deepest meeting of a lifetime as people are encouraged to persevere with the practical. There are few better ways to develop a climate in which sharing can grow.

Hospice, the team development of attitudes and skills to enhance the quality of life remaining, has been associated since the first home care programme was started in 1969 with 'living until you die' and with remaining at home as long as possible, if not to the very end. A death at home leaves a great sense of completion and achievement but no one should be made to feel guilty if this has finally to be in a hospice or hospital bed so long as the family continues to be involved and to be reassured that they did all they could and often a good deal more.

''If nurses or doctors say that they usually do not have problems with their dying patients it is because they have not recognised or acknowledged that the problems exist''. Many patients and families face complex distresses and there has to be constant analysis and effort on all sides. This book, so obviously written from experience and an unusual ability to learn even more from mistakes than from successes, will help all who are trying to enable those who desire it to have the chance of dying in their own home and those who care for them to have strengthening memories to support them in bereavement. From the first description of the assessment and analysis of pain, an essential component of successful home care, to a simple but detailed description of what dying is like at the end, here is a unique contribution to nursing literature, relevant not only to those involved in 'hospice' or 'continuing' or 'palliative' care but for all those who meet dying patients anywhere.

DAME CICELY SAUNDERS DBE FRCP
London 1983

Preface

There is an increasing deluge of publications concerning death, dying and bereavement, many of which include a chapter about home care of the patient and his family. This book is written entirely for those who care for patients at home. The aim is to provide practical information for everyday use. I have included accounts of some of my mistakes — in the hope that others might side-step them, to the benefit of those on the receiving end of care.

Drug regimes are considered in some detail. To be of maximum help to patients, it is necessary to be as thoroughly conversant with the pharmacological principles of the patient's medication as with other more traditional aspects of care. A multi-disciplinary team approach improves everyone's knowledge, which in turn improves patient care. For example, speedy relief is brought to the patient by a doctor who is willing to insert suppositories while visiting the patient, by a nurse who can adjust the level of analgesia within a specified range, or by a social worker who, during the course of a visit to discuss social problems, inquires about the patient's physical condition, and then communicates her concerns to the appropriate person for further action. Demarcation of role occurs at the acknowledged limits of one's own understanding and knowledge, or when someone more appropriate is *available* to fulfil a particular duty.

The content of this book is based on experience of nursing patients mainly suffering from carcinomatosis. However, many of the principles can be applied to other terminal conditions. The word 'terminal' appears very little in the text, because of the distorted view it has encouraged. Terminals relate to electric currents and computers. To hear a nurse say 'I've got two terminals', or 'When I have a terminal . . .', denies the wholeness of that patient in a similar manner to '. . . the varicose ulcer at No. 56', or '. . . the bronchus in bed 12'.

Hospice care is now available in many parts of the country. The addresses of some hospices are included at the end of the book in order that they may be approached for help or advice, and other useful addresses are also given.

For the sake of continuity and brevity, I have usually indicated patients and doctors in the masculine gender, and nurses in the feminine.

Throughout the text I have used several quotations from The Prophet by Kahlil Gibran, because of his ability to take the reader simply and directly to the heart of a subject. On teaching he says:

'No man can reveal to you aught but that which already lies half asleep in the dawning of your knowledge'.

How often we say 'ah, yes' in recognition and realization of something we are taught—whether by tutor or patient patient! I am sure there will be many nods of the head as this book is read.

HARRIET COPPERMAN
London 1983

Acknowledgements

The conclusion of any lecture given by me contains an acknowledgement of the lead and inspiration given by Dame Cicely Saunders in this work. On this occasion I shall start by thanking her for kindly supplying a Foreword for this book, as well as encouragement in the writing of it.

Dr Richard Lamerton provided unflagging help and support as he patiently rearranged some of my more dubious grammar and ideas. His limitless enthusiasm over the years, in conjunction with the comments and attitudes of many patients, have taught me so much.

I am grateful to Dr John Collins and Dr Peter Hardwick who helped me unravel the mysteries of the physiology of pain, and June Clark, Jean Greenshields, Julia Bard and Joyce Nash between them gave unlimited assistance, advice and encouragement to help me on my book-writing way.

HC

Introduction

'There's no place like home' is an old saying which is well understood by community nurses in relation to their patients, and indeed to their own job satisfaction.

For most people nearing the end of their life, home is a place they have known for perhaps 20–30 years. It is a place full of treasures gathered over many years, a place of pride, a place of rest and retreat from the world, a place of hospitality to others. From this home the passing of the seasons has been appreciated year after year in the garden as tenderly nurtured plants produce their tomatoes, beans, peas or flowers. The cat, dog or budgie plays its own part in the scenario. And, of course, the spouse who has shared all of this for the previous thirty, forty or even fifty years. What finer nurse can there be for a man who is dying, than the wife he has known all those years. She knows exactly how he likes his tea made, what would be the most tempting foods for his failing appetite and how to make him comfortable in his favourite armchair. Likewise many husbands can do the same for their wives.

This loving care combined with professional help from the primary health care team can enable many dying patients to remain at home so that they never have to experience the dread of being whisked away in an ambulance to the strange, often impersonal and frightening environment of hospital, where the dog and grandchildren are forbidden entry and the rest of the family may have only limited access.

It has now become generally accepted that many patients wish to die at home if possible, and that the home environment, even with some limitations, is for many the ideal place to die (Rees 1971).

A few generations ago it was assumed that most people would die in their own beds. The picture has now completely changed

1

and approximately 70% of the British population dies in some sort of institution. There is evidence, however, that this trend can be reversed. In 1975 the Macmillan Service at St Joseph's Hospice, London, was involved in the care of 263 dying patients. Throughout that first year the percentage dying at home rose from 39.3 to 55.6. In 1980–81 the number of patients was 453, 67% of whom died at home. A similar picture has been seen in some other units. These figures are used simply to illustrate the considerable potential for change.

Currently, the Department of Health and Social Security is recommending (at least in theory) that more resources be directed towards all aspects of community care, in recognition — long overdue — that the world exists outside, as well as inside, our hospitals. The efforts of Dr Gillian Ford (Ford & Pincherle 1978) and her colleagues at the Department of Health, combined with generous financial support from the National Society for Cancer Relief, have contributed greatly towards the provision of community care for dying patients.

Chapter 1

Assessments

The most important practical lesson that can be given to nurses is to teach them what to observe — how to observe . . .

Notes on Nursing. F. Nightingale

It is necessary to have a clear understanding of the needs of a situation before these needs can be answered. Careful assessment, not only of the patient, but also of the social and physical environment in which he lives, is vital.

Information gathered from the initial assessment enables immediate requirements to be satisfied and subsequent care properly planned — including some anticipation of likely problems and needs.

Assessment of Environment

As community nurses the first lesson we learn when carrying out our assessment of the patient's environment is not to judge or apply our own standards to our patients. Many an elderly lady who is 'at risk' is determined to stay in her 'castle' until she dies, however appalling we may consider the conditions. However, in many homes there are modifications which can be carried out to make a more practical and appropriate environment in which someone can die in peace and comfort.

Assessment of the home begins before entering it. What is the neighbourhood like — is it a friendly homely area or a lonely estate of high-rise buildings where most neighbours are out at work all day and are not interested in the problems of others? Is there an air of neglect outside the home and if so is it recent because of the illness inside or longstanding because of apathy, ignorance, the infirmity of old age or an uncaring landlord?

Inside the home an initial intuitive assessment is followed by one which is more thoughtful and analytical. One important consideration relates to the room to be used when the patient is close to death. While the patient is still mobile it is relatively simple for him to come downstairs by day and to go up again at night. Gradually the stairs become more difficult and eventually insurmountable. But if he then takes to his bed upstairs he may feel isolated from household activity, or the main care giver may become very tired from going up and down and anxious about what is happening to the patient when he is out of sight. In many homes it is possible to arrange for the patient to be nursed downstairs; this has several advantages for the very weak patient as it helps to prevent both his isolation and exhaustion of the care giver.

If, however, the patient is to be nursed downstairs, is there a suitable space for a bed? There will be times when the patient needs privacy and quiet and this may be difficult to provide if there is only one room downstairs, which serves as the gathering place for an avalanche of relatives of all ages. If there is space, is there a suitable bed? A settee is acceptable until the patient is close to death when it becomes very difficult to carry out adequate nursing procedures. What of the sleeping arrangements for the spouse? Sleeping in an armchair is all right for a night or so, but not for several weeks. If the spouse sleeps upstairs then there is the anxiety of leaving the patient at night. Finally, can suitable toilet arrangements be made? Is there a downstairs lavatory—or is it even outside? Will the patient accept a commode at that particular point in his illness?

There is another considerable advantage to having the patient sleep downstairs—after the death the spouse will not have to face what is for some the agony of sleeping in the bed in which the patient has died.

Other environmental factors such as heating, lighting, ventilation, hot water and laundry also need to be evaluated with the help of the main care giver.

Assessment of the Family

An article which describes the negative feeling of some nurses towards patients' relatives (Speck 1973) reminds me of my own ambivalent feelings as a student nurse when, for example, relatives would bring masses of flowers for which vases had to be found: then the flowers were overturned whenever the curtains were pulled round the patient's bed. Relatives also wanted to ask questions and their presence had the effect of untidying a geometrically organized ward!

At home it is rapidly realized and acknowledged that the spouse or main care giver(s) is the crucial factor which may or may not enable the patient to die at home. So it is vital to assess the family's ability to cope. The oft-repeated 'hospice care is family care' is generally more easily recognized and practised by staff working in the community.

This assessment also begins before entering the home. What happens when the door-bell is rung—is there an instant din from barking dogs and children, or a long pause followed by the sound of some elderly relative shuffling to answer the door? How is the greeting by that person—eyes cast downward, a welcoming smile, a look of relief, or a look of fear, anxiety and exhaustion?

Often the spouse's anxiety is expressed as soon as the door is opened: 'He doesn't know what he's got. Don't tell him, it would kill him'. An explanation that the patient probably has a good idea what's happening already, that he will not be told anything he does not want to hear, and that he will probably tell us about his diagnosis, not vice versa, can usually diminish these fears and lay the foundation for total communication between patient, family and professionals during the coming weeks.

During the course of the visit the nurse must ascertain how much family or neighbourly support the main care giver is likely to receive. Are the grown-up children able or willing to lend a hand as necessary? If there is no family, will the neighbours help the spouse—even by coming in for a cup of tea and a chat? Is the spouse retired from work, or able to take compassionate leave without losing his/her employment? A letter from a professional, thanking an employer for being so considerate and understanding in the circumstances, may be more effective than a letter requesting compassionate leave. Is the spouse physically active or restricted by arthritis or chronic heart or lung disease? If there is not one main care giver, will it be possible for the family to organize and maintain a rota in order to care for the patient?

The ability of the spouse to cope will also be affected by his/her mental and emotional state and capacity. There are some homes where the death of a close relative has never been experienced and where such a prospect may be intolerable. Conversely, some families may have had to cope with several deaths within a short time and the approach of another death at home may be just too much to contemplate.

Some families want to manage, others do not. If the patient has provoked ill-feeling in his lifetime the relatives may not wish to make more than a token effort at looking after him. At the other end of the spectrum, a warm and loving family may often move heaven and earth to deal with the situation. Some families can manage miracles provided it is not for too long. The disruption of lifestyles may reach breaking point if the patient's disease runs a chronic course over months or years, which can happen if the cancer is slow-growing, particularly in some elderly patients, or if the patient is dying of another condition which generally runs a chronic course, such as bronchitis and emphysema.

Assessment of the Patient

Assessment of the patient is so important because his attitude and approach to life, rather than medical or nursing problems, could prevent him from dying at home. Our senses and level of awareness must be keenly focused throughout the whole of the visit and assessment, but particularly when with the patient.

Is he for example sitting in a chair in a position isolated from the remainder of the room, so that either verbal or physical contact is inhibited? Is his welcome genuine or a facade behind which lies fear (of hospitalization), anger (at yet more people interfering in his life), indifference (due to depression), frustration (because of his dependence on others), anxiety (the arrival of the nurse means I am probably quite ill)? Is he being polite in his welcome by forcing himself to be lively, when in fact he sleeps most of the time and is making a special effort for the nurse's visit? How does he appear to relate to his spouse or main care giver? Patients frequently become very frustrated as they realize that the body taken for granted over the past 50, 60 or 70 years, no longer responds in the usual way; these frustrations are often transferred to other family members in the form of bad-tempered behaviour, which in turn may set up intolerable tensions in the home.

Our senses will tell us much more. Using our eyes will reveal a great deal about the patient's state. He may look anxious, angry and depressed, or satisfied, contented and serene. Are his hands clenched, brow furrowed and body moving frequently or continuously, perhaps indicating that he is in pain? Is he lying very still in order not to stir up a pain, dyspnoea or nausea? Does he have a tremor of his hands which could perhaps be a side effect of some medication? Are his finger-nails long and unkempt? Does he look confused—or appear so because he is in fact deaf?

Without using a stethoscope, the sense of hearing may reveal that the patient has or is developing a chest infection, or has bronchospasm. Bowel sounds heard loud and clear in the room may indicate constipation or threatening intestinal obstruction. Is the patient's voice husky? If he has a carcinoma of the bronchus it is probably from a recurrent laryngeal nerve palsy, or it may mean monilial infection of the mouth and/or larynx. Does he have difficulty speaking because of a dry mouth caused by medication containing opiates or phenothiazines, or dehydration?

The sense of touch when shaking the patient's hand may reveal anxiety (cold and clammy), pyrexia (hot and sweaty) or even thyrotoxicosis. Is the handshake firm and strong or limp and weak? Is the skin dry and dehydrated?

Many closely guarded secrets may be revealed by using the sense of smell. A smell of stale urine could indicate that the patient (or spouse) has urinary incontinence problems. Passing frequent flatus is likely to result from constipation. Then there is the unfortunate and unmistakable odour of advanced carcinoma of cervix or uterus and of malignant ulceration and infection of a breast tumour. The patient's embarrassment must be allayed as much as possible during the visit, assisted by reassurance that the smell can probably be controlled. The nose may also diagnose an unclean or infected mouth or the smell of liver failure ('mousey') or renal failure (fishy + ammonia) on the breath. Recent vomit, especially haematemesis, has a distinctive odour. Another all-pervading smell may be the scent of artificial roses or violets as an anxiously houseproud wife wildly and enthusiastically sprays chemical aerosol at everyone and everything, to produce what she believes to be a sweet-smelling atmosphere.

Following the initial assessment by the senses, most of which occurs during the first minutes after entering the house and greeting the patient, comes the more systematic assessment based on verbal communication. In order to be able to care effectively for the patient a fairly detailed history is needed, and it would be a courtesy to warn him that it is necessary to ask a considerable number of questions. It is also important to remember to give attention to the patient and not just to a list of questions on numerous sheets of paper which are filled

Fig 1

in with great haste. How well Sheena Best's cartoon (Fig 1) illustrates this point! (This cartoon, reproduced by kind permission of the Editor of the *Nursing Mirror*, was drawn by Sheena Best.)

Nurses may feel that the gathering of some of this history should be carried out by the general practitioner. However, there are many occasions in the community when the nurse might visit the patient before the doctor — such as following discharge from hospital. In order to facilitate and organize appropriate care the sooner the facts are gathered the better it is for the patient.

Too often in the past a district nurse has been asked to visit a patient for a 'breast dressing' or 'colostomy care' and after performing such tasks feels that that is all that is needed. The nursing process can certainly be used to dislodge these old habits, but we must guard against substituting another habit, equally inflexible. This means that the information gathered must not be just a form-filling and form-filing exercise to satisfy the employing authority. The only justification for collecting information is to make good use of it. If the forms seem inappropriate then we must press for them to be improved — not just sigh and continue with an unsatisfactory system.

An Outline of Information Required

Occupation

Some industrial diseases, such as mesothelioma caused by working with asbestos, are notifiable. Many patients who have mesothelioma are eligible for compensation. (SPAID is an organization set up to help such patients with their claims — see Appendix 2.)

Religion

It is not enough to note that the patient's religion is 'C of E', or whatever it may be. As death approaches it is important to know how much his religion means to the patient or, indeed, whether he wishes to discuss it at all. Distress and embarrassment can be prevented by ascertaining this early in the relationship. The sort of response elicited from such questions as 'Do you know your vicar?' or 'Have you been to church lately?' will usually give a fairly clear indication about his views on the matter.

Family

It is helpful to know the names and ages of young children in the home, so that a relationship can be established with them, and to be alerted to possible future problems for a single-parent family and bereavement of children. Addresses and telephone numbers of grown-up children should be noted, in order that they may be contacted either to receive information or be asked for it — perhaps clarifying interfamily relationships, which can be quite explosive! Building up a family tree on paper may provide a useful visual aid.

Other contacts

In order that care may be co-ordinated and not duplicated, names and telephone numbers should be collected of other visitors to the house. For example, a social worker, health visitor or home help may already be involved. It may be useful to enquire about the schooling of any children, so that their teachers can be informed about the problems in the home — or likely ones — if the parents have not already done so. A note should be taken of the hospital the patient attends, the name of the consultant(s) and the dates of future appointments.

History of the illness

This need only be brief but it can be a helpful way of encouraging the patient (if he needs it) to talk and of assessing what knowledge he has of his diagnosis. For example, if asked what the operation was for or why radiotherapy was given, the reply may indicate knowledge of his condition, denial of it or genuine ignorance about it. A history enables evaluation of the possibility of further treatment, if, for example, the patient was told he could have no further radiotherapy to a specific area.

Current medication

This should be carefully noted. It is often an excellent opportunity to advise a family about discarding old supplies of tablets which have accumulated over half a lifetime! It is also essential to check very carefully if the patient and/or relatives understand what he should be taking currently, and when. It is not uncommon for a patient to be discharged from hospital on a myriad of different pills and potions to be taken at different times. If in doubt, he will either take them randomly or not at all.

Systems and symptoms

Digestive system

Appetite—Is his appetite good, bad or indifferent? Are there any specific factors which affect it, such as an inexperienced family member preparing unappetizing food?

Nausea—Is it continuous or intermittent? Does it arise at a particular time, for example after taking analgesic medication?

Vomiting—What does it look like? When does it happen and how often? How much is vomited each time and does it have any particular features such as the smell of faeces or projectile in nature?

Hiccoughs—When do they occur and how long do they persist?

Dysphagia—Is it partial or total? Which foods go down and which do not? Is it helped by medication? Is it accompanied by waterbrash?

Bowel function—A very critical assessment is essential here. If a patient says his bowels are satisfactory, it is necessary to verify that by asking when he last had a bowel movement, was it normal or hard like rabbit pellets? Did he pass as much as usual? I cannot over-emphasize the considerable degree of profound constipation caused by analgesia and missed so often by doctors and nurses. Similar close questioning should be applied if the patient says he has diarrhoea.

Respiratory system

Dyspnoea—This may cause more distress to the patient than pain. Is he more comfortable sitting up or lying down? To what degree is he dyspnoeic?
Cough—Is it productive or dry? When is it worse—by day or night? Does it disturb sleep? If there is sputum what is it like— tenacious, yellow, green, red or brown?

Circulatory system

Embolus—Does the patient have any history of deep vein thrombosis, phlebitis or varicose veins? Has he had a myocardial infarction, angina or cerebrovascular accident?
Pacemaker—If the patient has a pacemaker in situ it must be removed prior to cremation to avoid an EXPLOSION.

Genito-urinary system

Micturition—Is it normal or painful? Is there a problem with nocturia frequency or haematuria (the urine may be coloured red as a result of taking the laxative Dorbanex)? Is the patient continent by day and night?

Nervous system (including mental state)

Headache—Is this a new symptom or has he had migraines all his life?
Pain—See Chapter 2.
Paralysis, paresis or paraesthesiae—These may indicate the likely site of metastases. If mobility is impaired—to what degree has it occurred and how rapidly? How well do the patient and family cope with it? Does the patient need or allow help with washing himself, shaving and moving?
Level of consciousness—Is the level of consciousness normal or is he excessively drowsy? Does he sleep normally or complain that he only sleeps for an hour or so at night? What was his normal sleep pattern? . . .
Speech—Does it sound slurred, perhaps caused by medication

or cerebral metasteses, quiet as a result of weakness, hoarse as a result of monilial infection? Does the patient complain of difficulty in using the right words?

Anxiety or Depression — This may not be demonstrated clearly at the first visit. Some impression can be gained by the patient's response to questions concerning his sleep pattern, his interest in daily life, his ability to concentrate on reading or his favourite hobbies, how he sees the future or simply by asking if he is worried or depressed.

Skin

Discharge — There may be a discharge from a wound or any orifice, for example, a nasal discharge from a maxilliary tumour.

Pressure areas — Has the patient any complaint or soreness or history of broken skin over heels, hips, buttocks, etc?

Rashes (or irritation) — Does the patient have a record of drug allergy, perhaps to antibiotics or Dorbanex?

Weight loss — Has the patient noticed a change in weight recently? Patients often point to skin hanging in folds where weight has been lost.

Oedema — (a) of the arm, which may be the result of a radical mastectomy in the past or (b) of the lower limbs, which may result from a degree of cardiac failure, from pelvic obstruction by a tumour, or as a result of the use of steroids.

Special senses

Hearing — Is deafness a problem that the patient is not aware of? Is it related to what the patient does or does not want to hear? Does he need a new hearing-aid or have a problem with his current one? Has he ever needed to have his ears syringed?

Sight — A patient with advanced cancer will often complain of deteriorating vision. Diplopia might indicate a cerebral secondary.

Taste — Sometimes a patient will report a bad taste which affects everything he eats or drinks.

Smell — Complaints of unusual or absent smells may indicate a cerebral metastasis.

The list of questions can become almost endless, but with practice much of the information is gathered in a conversational manner while also establishing the relationship.

A simple physical examination by the nurse can then be carried out. This should include checking the mouth with a torch (and at subsequent visits), for signs of monilial infection (thrush), which is a common cause of distress to many patients. At the time time it will be obvious from the condition of the buccal mucosa whether or not the patient is dehydrated.

The abdomen may be inspected for obvious signs of ascites. If the abdomen is emaciated and concave, gentle palpation may reveal (with just a bit of practice) lumps in the left iliac fossa which are not peritoneal metastases but faeces (faeces are squashable when pressed). Gentle palpation and percussion might show the presence of urinary retention should it be suspected. If there is any possibility of constipation or if the patient complains of diarrhoea the rectum should be examined. The index finger may collide with hard faeces or a faecal impaction producing an overflow diarrhoea. It is also possible that a tumour mass may be felt either inside or outside the rectum, thereby occasionally revealing the site of a tumour in a patient who had been previously diagnosed as having carcinomatosis from an unknown primary. Rectal examination can also facilitate rapid inspection of the sacral and other pressure areas. At the same time any rash on or around the buttocks can be noted—the patient may not have known about it or not bothered to mention it.

The condition of the pressure areas around the feet should be observed, as well as any ankle, leg or sacral oedema.

The site of wounds, drains, colostomy or other intervention to the patient's body should be inspected and the patient questioned about his management of them.

If the patient has been seen recently by his general practitioner it may not be necessary for the nurse to cover the same ground again. Nevertheless, conversation with the patient should incorporate continuous reappraisal of the situation, bearing in mind all the factors and aspects that have been outlined. When someone has perhaps only a few weeks left to live, his condition can vary rapidly from day to day. It is our job to be alert and watching for these changes, so that relief for the patient can be quickly obtained. IF NURSES OR DOCTORS SAY THAT THEY USUALLY DO NOT HAVE PROBLEMS WITH THEIR DYING PATIENTS IT IS BECAUSE THEY HAVE NOT RECOGNIZED OR ACKNOWLEDGED THAT THE PROBLEMS EXIST.

It is also worth remembering that while many patients love the opportunity to answer questions and talk repeatedly about their illness, others do not. Communication with the medical practitioner(s) involved, either before or after the visit (or both), is important so that information gathered by either party can be exchanged.

I remember visiting a patient who had recently come under our care who retorted angrily 'You are the fourth person to ask me these questions'. Obviously, and especially in the early stages of the relationship, it is important not to have too many new faces thrust at a patient. This can be difficult if there are staff shortages, annual leave or sickness, but that effort should be made, particularly for the first week or two.

An opportunity should also be given for the patient to ask any questions or make any comments. At the first meeting he may decline the offer—probably because it has never been made to him before. However, from that he will know that he can take up the option on another occasion when he has marshalled his thoughts.

The gathering of all this information at initial assessment can take an hour or more, which may seem a lot of time to a community nurse with a large caseload, but it lays a very firm foundation for a relationship which must be established if the nurse is to win the trust and confidence of the patient and family. This trust will enable the nurse to be much more effective in the coming weeks, than if she had breezed in, changed the breast dressing and hurried out again.

Chapter 2

Pain and its Management

And could you keep your heart in wonder at the daily miracles of your
life, your pain would not seem less wondrous than your joy . . .

The Prophet K Gibran

That is an attitude which few of us are able to achieve for
anything but the briefest of moments. Physical pain is usually
something most people want alleviated as soon as possible. It is
in acknowledgement of this fact that this chapter comes before
others which are more usually considered to be within the
province of the nurse.

Pain, unpleasant as it is, is of course an important protective
factor for the health of the body. It acts as a warning bell in
many situations — such as toothache, the pain of arthritic joints,
backache or full bladder. Without these warnings the body
would deteriorate and die much more quickly. The imminent
birth of a baby is heralded by labour pains. All such aches and
pains appear to be useful and to some degree therefore,
acceptable. However, to most patients the pain of cancer seems
very different. It is frightening because of the ideas, prevalent in
society, of dying in screaming agony as the cancer rampages
through the body. The pain of cancer also appears to the patient
to serve no useful purpose, unlike the warnings given by other
pains. Cancer pain envelopes and overwhelms the patient so that
he is unable to partake wholeheartedly in the life he has left to
live. It is experienced, albeit with some diurnal variation (Glyn et
al. 1976), 24 hours a day, 7 days a week.

Fortunately, nurses are becoming more aware of the meaning
of pain to the patient, although full appreciation is still some
way off (Hunt *et al.* 1977). Sadly, the medical profession
continues to lag far behind in the awareness of the desperation
and loneliness produced by pain, which occurs in 50–60% of

patients with cancer (Saunders 1981). This awareness is vital: without it there is no motivation to improve the situation. Far too frequently we meet a patient with a distressing story of having been in pain for months on end. As an aid to help some doctors understand pain, one very non-professional idea frequently springs to mind, but which I have so far resisted. The manoeuvre would be, literally, to stamp on a dilatory medical foot and point out that the pain experienced is comparable with that suffered by a patient in pain!

Another difficulty in the appreciation of pain is that unlike other symptoms, such as vomiting, cough or anaesthesia it cannot be watched, quantified or scientifically demonstrated. Pain, because it will not appear on expensive, sophisticated, computerized scanning equipment, is deemed unworthy of attention. *Pain is what the patient says it is*, however we may decide to treat it.

I believe it is the duty of every district nurse not to give in to a dismissive general practitioner until she has obtained relief for her patient. Nowadays most of the pain of cancer can be totally or partially relieved. There are occasionally patients who, for spiritual reasons, wish to experience pain, but most religious leaders advocate relief of physical pain except for the few ascetics who can make use of it. Engraved in my memory is a patient I was looking after before I had been enlightened about pain control. He obviously only had a few days to live and was in great pain. The general practitioner—an otherwise competent, caring and effective doctor—refused to prescribe anything but minor analgesia. The pain he said was psychological. The patient died in agony two days later, devotedly cared for by a distraught wife. We must do everything we can to prevent such disasters. Torture *is* alive and well in the Western World: every day all over our civilized cities—with all the wonders we have discovered and created, people are still dying appallingly through ignorance, apathy and neglect. An American physician claimed that a visitor to St Christopher's Hospice in London had been shown only the patients who were least ill (Lau 1981).

It cost Lister many difficult and frustrating years to convince the world about antisepsis. Today we can hardly believe in the ignorance and attitudes of the time. Perhaps in not too many more years as we as a society will regard the relief of pain and suffering similarly. Dame Cicely Saunders has been spreading this message for the major part of her professional life.

The Physiology of Pain

Much work has been done in recent years to try to comprehend this aspect of physiology. However, the more that is discovered the more questions arise from these discoveries (Melzack & Wall 1965). The following section is, therefore, a greatly simplified outline and introduction to the subject.

The differences between the acute pain of a burn and the chronic pain of cancer, can to some extent, be explained by differences in known physiological mechanisms. However, these mechanisms do not account for the wide spectrum of pain intensity experienced; psychological and psychochemical factors are also of importance in determining an individual's pain sensitivity at any one time.

All tissues have pain receptors, some more than others. For example a square inch of finger will be more sensitive than the same size of liver. Pain receptors in the body consist of free nerve endings. They are widespread in the skin surfaces and certain internal tissues such as periosteum, joints, parietal pleura and peritoneum. These receptors are present in lesser concentration in most other tissues.

The nerve endings may be stimulated by the release of a variety of chemical substances, such as prostaglandins, which occurs when tissues are damaged. Some of these chemicals are inhibited by simple analgesics such as aspirin and this fact goes some way towards explaining the useful effects of such drugs.

Pain signals from the nerve endings in the tissues are transmitted to the spinal cord and brain by two different types of nerve fibres—fast or delta fibres and slow or C fibres. The fast fibres are important in acute pain, initiating immediate reaction to prevent further damage. The C fibres are less obviously useful, carrying a slow burning sensation. They are presumed to be more active in chronic pain and predominate in the nerve supply to internal organs. On the whole, acute pains tend to have less psycho-reactive components; this may be due to specific differences in nervous pathways.

Pain fibres of both types enter the spinal cord through the sensory (dorsal) nerve roots and within the cord they are connected—with one or two short nerve cells in between—to long fibres which pass upwards to the brain. These spinal inter-connections allow modification of the pain signals as they pass through the cord; simultaneous signals are transmitted to the cord from other parts of the body or from the brain itself. This is called the 'gate control'. The basic concept is that the 'gate' is either open or closed—either pain or not pain. The word 'gate' is used by electrophysicists to mean an electrical switch. It is the probable explanation for the common experience that pain intensity is altered by other stimuli—physical or psychological. Gate control also explains, in part, the mode of action of various physical analgesics such as applied heat, acupuncture and transcutaneous electrical nerve stimulation. Similar mechanisms may be involved in the actions of centrally-acting analgesics such as opiates. A simple diagram will help explain all this (Fig 2).

For simplicity the idealized spinal cord cell shown in Fig 2 has four connections: 1 is the axon or main conducting fibre, travelling to the brain; 2 a synapse with another adjacent cell; 3 a synapse with a sensory nerve cell receiving signals from its ending say in the skin, and 4 is a second motor connection indirectly via other nerve cells coming from the brain. These connections represent the switches or 'gates'. In the simplest circumstance a painful stimulus will activate synapse 3: this excites the cell which conducts its signal to the brain—transmitting the 'pain' to conscious awareness.

If synapse 2 is also excited at the same time, for example by acupuncture, the pain signal may be inhibited, diminished or pass unnoticed altogether depending on the various inter-connections. Other connections may therefore control the 'gate' —in reality these connections are abundant.

Similarly, the use of opiate drugs which become bonded to specific opiate receptors in the brain and cord (Lewis1978) may give rise to activity (or inactivity) at synapse 3. This will again alter transmission of the pain signal.

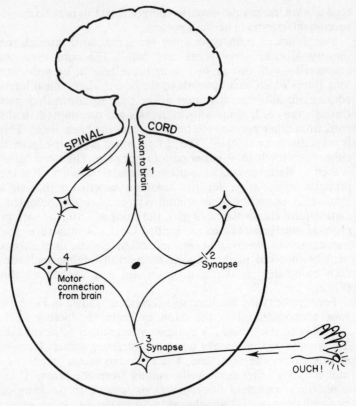

Fig 2   Diagram of pain pathways

It has become apparent recently that the body manufactures chemicals such as endorphins (Hill 1981), similar to opiate analgesics, which are active at the opiate receptors in the brain and spinal cord and which play a part in the modification of pain (Br. Med. J. 1980). These receptors are known to modify the sensation of pain and such simple acts as massaging a painful area, supplying heat or more complex stimuli such as acupuncture, may all in fact operate by increasing endogenous endorphin secretion. Opiate drugs work presumably by mimicking endorphin activity at receptor sites — closing the 'gate'.

There is much research work in progress throughout the world, including the United Kingdom, on the manufacture of endorphins. It may be that in the future we shall be in a better position to modify the pain experience of a patient, either by chemical or physical (eg. electro-energy means). This, then, will open up the scope of methods of pain relief which until the present time have been somewhat limited because of our ignorance of the more complicated mechanisms of pain.

The Assessment of Pain

Before considering how to treat pain it is necessary to know the nature of it and to realize that there can be many causes of pain in a patient with cancer, other than the cancer itself. First of all, an accurate picture of the pain is needed. There may be more than one pain — often after relieving one overwhelming pain, the patient becomes aware of several others (Twycross 1978a). It is important to ask the patient for the precise site of the pain. Dr Robert Twycross in Oxford uses a body chart in the notes so that the exact location is indicated (Fig 3).

For example, the patient may complain of pain in the chest. Is there a tender spot on the ribs which could indicate a bony metastasis which might respond to radiotherapy or a nerve block? Does it radiate round indicating perhaps a collapsing thoracic vertebra, or is the pain in a distinct band revealing perhaps the presence of shingles (herpes zoster)? Perhaps the pain feels as though it is right inside the chest, or is associated with respiration. There are so many possibilities for just one pain. We must be able to pick out as many clues as possible in this most serious detective game, in order that the doctor may make an accurate diagnosis of the cause of the pain and hence provide appropriate treatment.

Other qualities relating to the pain should also be elicited. Is it a dull pain or sharp like a knife? Does it come and go in crescendos of colic, perhaps caused by constipation? Is the pain gripping and vice-like? Is it related to a particular activity, such as eating or lying down? Is it worse at night or at any other time? Do different positions make it worse or relieve it? It is also essential to remember that some patients do not perceive their

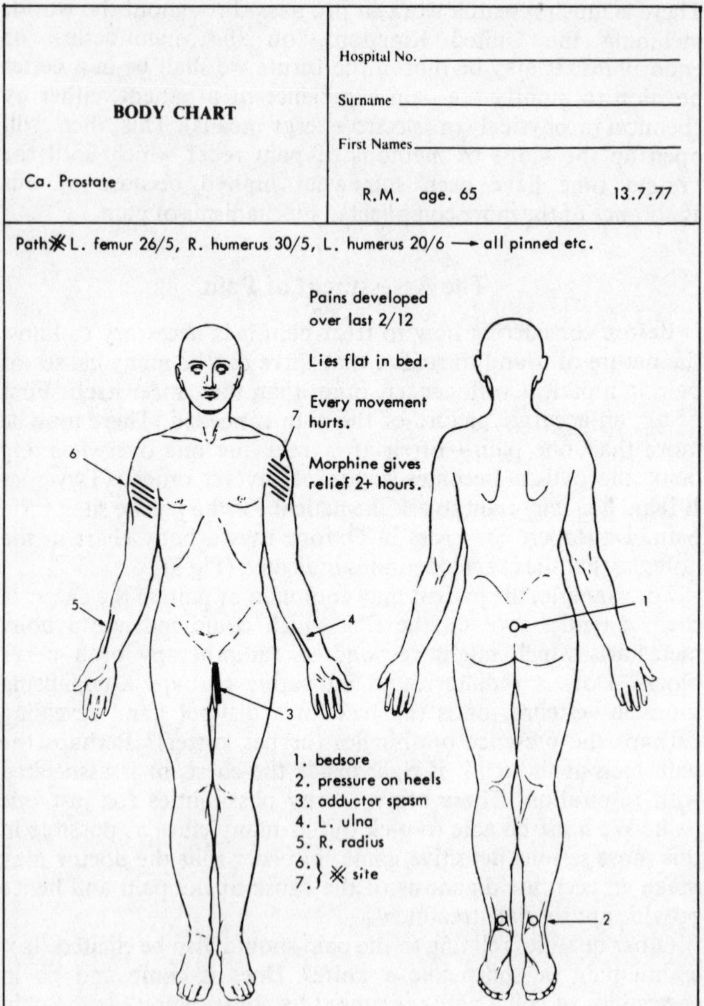

Fig 3   Body chart. (Reproduced by courtesy of Pitman Books Limited, London, from *Topics in Therapeutics*, Volume 4.)

feeling of tightness and discomfort around, say, their chest, as pain. If asked whether they have pain they will reply in the negative, so that obviously precise attention must be given to hear what the patient is saying.

Non-Cancerous Causes of Pain

Arthritic. This may mimic bony secondaries.

Cardiac. It can be easy to miss a myocardial infarction if the patient has a bronchial carcinoma likely to cause pain.

Pleuritic. This also may be ascribed wrongly to a carcinoma.

Embolic. I remember one occasion when it took several days to realize that a patient's exacerbating chest pain was not responding to increased analgesia as expected, because the pain was in fact from a pulmonary embolus and not his tumour.

Phlebitis and deep vein thrombosis.

Intestinal obstruction. This, too, is frequently caused by constipation. We have seen patients die of constipation, having been referred too late for adequate treatment.

Bladder infection or distention. This can be easily missed if the pain is assumed to be caused by carcinoma of the bladder or of that region.

Haemorrhoids. Can cause considerable pain which may not be fully appreciated by care givers, especially if modesty should make the patient reluctant to disclose the problem.

Pressure sores. At the superficial stage these may cause considerable discomfort.

Gastric ulceration. This may be a side effect of treatment, for example with steroids.

Nocturnal cramps. Life can be very wearisome if cramps are severe, by preventing the patient from having adequate rest.

Infection. However large or small, this it can be very painful. In fact, we know from our own experience that the smallest pinprick or pimple can cause a lot of discomfort, so we must be vigilant to our patients' complaints.

Toenails. These appear to have become unfashionable of late and dealing with them is deemed not to be a nursing duty: consequently, some patients experience great pain and distress from long curling toenails digging mercilessly into their flesh. Such neglect by nurses is inexcusable, particularly in areas where there are inadequate chiropody services.

(A salutory tale). A patient with a cerebral tumour referred following hospital discharge had two complaints (apart from his headache). He wanted his last two remaining teeth removed because they were loose and cutting into his lip causing it to bleed; and he had a corn, the pain from which kept him awake at night. One can speculate on the reasons why these were not attended to whilst the patient was in hospital (his wife, the main care giver, was disabled from a stroke). Perhaps the staff *were* too busy. Perhaps, though, such symptoms were judged to be insignificant.

Pains from Cancer

Skull.   Pain or headache are likely from a primary or
Cerebral. secondary tumour.

Backache. This may be caused by involvement of one or many vertebrae.

Nerve compression. May produce agonizing girdle pain or shooting pain down the limbs.

Long bones. The pain may be from a primary or secondary tumour or pathological fracture.

Chest. This pain may be external or internal or both.

Abdomen. May be stretched by ascites or contain painful secondaries.

Liver. Can be an excrutiating pain as the liver capsule is stretched by metastases.

Visceral. Caused by tumours of other abdominal organs.

Intestine, bile duct or ureter. Severe colic may be associated with these tumours.

Rectum. Tormenting tenesmus may arise from rectal tumours.

Many ways of eliminating or at least considerably reducing pain have been evolved in recent years. Sometimes only one form of treatment is necessary, but on other occasions many different approaches have to be made in order to make the patient comfortable.

Pain is a subjective experience and as previously mentioned cannot be quantitatively analysed. Consider for example the variation of intensity of pain experienced by women in labour. This can range from almost no discomfort from an obviously contracting uterus, to an excrutiating extreme.

Pain perception or threshold can be affected by several factors and thus, in a dying patient, will influence the amount of analgesia required. Lack of sleep, perhaps caused by pain, can affect many patients. Anxiety, depression, the stress of social problems and environment may lower pain threshold. Also significant would be the patient's general approach to life before the illness: some people have had many difficult experiences and coped well, others have run away from problems and difficulties and not tolerated them.

Currently there is an increasing number of analgesics available and there is a certain amount of controversy about their efficacy. However (at the moment), there is universal agreement among hospice workers that pentazocine (Fortral) and pethidine have no place in the management of cancer pain, and dextro-moramide (Palfium) has a very limited role, where short-acting analgesia is required—perhaps when carrying out a painful procedure such as a difficult dressing.

| NAME MR. I.M. HAPPY | | DATE 3·3·83 | |
TIME	NAME OF DRUG	DESCRIPTION OF DRUG	DOSE
10am	MST	Purple pain tablet	1 tablet
	Stemetil	Small white sickness tablet	1 tablet
	Benoral	White pain medicine	2 tea spoons
	Vibramycin	Green antibiotic capsule	1 capsule
10pm	MST		1 tablet
	Stemetil		1 tablet
	Benoral		2 tea spoons
	Dorbanex Forte	Orange bowel medicine	2 tea spoons
	Valium	Yellow sleeping tablet	1-2 tablets

Fig 4   12-hour drug card

The aim of analgesia is to eliminate physical pain around the clock, while leaving the patient as alert and functional as possible. Medication which has to be given more frequently than 4-hourly imposes an unrealistic strain on patient compliance. The patient may have weeks, months or even years left to live. It is our duty to increase the likelihood of co-operation from the patient. Thus, in a domiciliary situation one of the aims is to reduce as much as possible the frequency and volume of medication. We are all too familiar with the confusion caused to patient and family by doctors who prescribe multiple medications—some daily, some three times a day, some with food, some before or after and some when there is an R in the month! With the wide range of medication available today, many drugs can be given 12-hourly. Being easier for the patient to manage, a 12-hourly regime is likely considerably to reduce wastage and overspending.

A useful way of helping the patient to understand what and when he should be taking is to write it out on a card (Fig 4). This may take five or ten minutes, but if it is done hurriedly and illegibly it will be a waste of time because the patient will not understand it or use it.

Commonly Used Analgesics

—including non-steroidal anti-inflammatory drugs (Twycross 1978b), opiates and strong synthetic analgesics.

Aspirin 300 mg
2 tablets 4-hourly
—Cheap and very useful, but beware gastric irritation. Soluble form available. Good anti-inflammatory action.

Choline magnesium trisalicylate 500 mg (Trilisate) 2–3 tablets 12-hourly
—12-hourly administration useful. It is fairly well tolerated.

Benorylate suspension 4 g/10 ml (Benoral) 10 mls 12-hourly
—Similar to aspirin and useful for patients at home because of twice daily administration. It is expensive, but thought to be better tolerated than aspirin.

Paracetamol 500 mg
(Panadol)
2 tablets 4-hourly
—Does not produce gastric side effects, but the tablets may be too large for some people to swallow when weak.

Codeine phosphate
8 mg + soluble aspirin
500 mg (Codis)
2 tablets 4-hourly
in water
—Very effective analgesic, but beware constipation. Weak opiate.

Dihydrocodeine
30 mg (DF 118)
1–2 tablets 4-hourly
—Approximately twice the strength of codeine.

Dextropropoxyhene
32.5 mg + paracetamol
325 mg (Distalgesic)
2 tablets 4-hourly
—Easy to swallow. Popular with many patients. Soluble variety less acceptable because of its taste.

Indomethacin 25 or
50 mg (Indocid)
75–150 mg daily
—Used for its anti-inflammatory action. Also available as a slow release capsule (75 mg) for use once or twice daily.

Diflunisal 250 mg
(Dolobid)
1–2 tablets 12-hourly
—Anti-inflammatory action. There is a 500 mg tablet, but would be too large for many people to swallow.

Buprenorphine 0.2 mg
(Temgesic)
1–3 tablets 6–8 hourly,
sublingually
—Morphine agonist/antagonist, so should not be used in conjunction with opiates. Limited use. May need to be taken with an antiemetic. Available as an injection (0.3 mg/ml). Advantage is of being a non-controlled drug.

If these analgesics do not adequately contain the patient's pain then stronger medication may be necessary:

Dipipanone 10 mg +
Cyclizine 30 mg
(Diconal)
1–2 tablets 4-hourly
—Good analgesic but the cyclizine often causes unwelcome drowsiness. Try half a tablet as initial dose to judge effect. Not currently prescribed very frequently in hospices.

Phenazocine 5 mg
(Narphen)
—Very potent analgesic—approximately 3 times that of diamorphine. Small,

1–2 tablets 4–6-hourly	easy-to-swallow tablet. May be used sublingually (Bullingham & McQuay 1981). Can be useful when the patient is unable to swallow, but is very bitter.
Methadone 5 mg (Physeptone) 6–8-hourly	—(See p.31 for dosage) Available in 10 mg/ml solution for injection. Main disadvantage is the cumulative effect and long plasma half life of probably several days (Ettinger *et al.* 1979). Used more in the U.S.A. than elsewhere. It can be used as an opiate substitute by the small number (less than 2%) of patients who hypereact to morphine with hallucinations or nightmares. Useful if injections are needed in the last day or so.
Oxycodone pectinate 30 mf (Formerly Proladone) 1–2 suppositories 8–12 hourly	—Very useful in domicilary work, when the patient is unable to take oral medication.

	Approximate Equivalents	Morphine	*Dia-morphine*
Dipipanone	10 mg (one tablet)	4 mg	3 mg
Dihydrocodeine	30 mg (one tablet)	5 mg	2.5 mg
Methadone	5 mg (one tablet)	7.5 mg	5 mg
Oxycodone	30 mg (one suppository)	20 mg	15 mg
Phenazocine	5 mg (one tablet)	22.5 mg	15 mg

Opiates and Strong Synthetic Analgesics

Much has been written and said about this group of drugs, but it is well worth restating as there is obviously still considerable resistance to their use. I have been involved for more than seven years in the routine use of strong analgesics and can only conclude that many commonly-used medications such as aspirin, insulin and digoxin are infinitely more deserving of the name 'dangerous drug' than morphine and similar substances.

Having participated in the care of several thousand patients, many of whom were regularly receiving opiates, I have rarely seen a patient demanding and craving ever-increasing doses (Twycross, 1982). Occasionally a patient would be referred to us in that condition, but a steady oral regime could even then usually be adopted.

It is important to realize that as the disease progresses the pain may increase, thus necessitating larger doses of analgesia. This obviously does not mean that the patient is an addict. Some patients in fact do not need dose changes. I remember Mrs R., a 32 year old lady who was on 20 mg oral diamorphine 4-hourly until she died of her cancer 3 years later. Every time we tried to lower her dose her pain returned, but we never needed to raise it either.

Physical dependence does occur after several weeks as it does when a patient is taking steroids. In *exactly* the same manner as steroids, if a patient does not require opiates any longer — perhaps because the pain has remitted following a dose of radio-therapy — there is *no* difficulty whatsoever in tailing off the dose (Vere 1978), usually over a few weeks, depending on the dose to be reduced. Society does not consider a patient on steroids to be an addict. Oral analgesics are no different. 'Addiction' means a psychological state of dependence; it simply never arises with oral medication.

It is important also to understand that very few patients who are conscious require analgesia administered in any way other than orally. Dosages throughout this text refer to oral preparations unless specified otherwise.

Analgesics do have one serious side effect — gut motility is reduced which causes CONSTIPATION (Lamerton 1978). Respiratory depression rarely causes problems, and indeed can be helpful in the treatment of dyspnoea in a dying patient.

Another strongly held idea is that opiates and other strong analgesics hasten death. Measurement of such an effect is obviously difficult, but from experience it appears that by relieving pain the patients are enabled to participate in life again and often seem to live longer than might have been expected when they were referred initially for palliative care.

The response of an elderly patient to such medication must be watched very carefully, and dose increases made more slowly than with the younger age groups (in this context 'elderly' may generally be considered to be 80+ years). Initially, many patients will experience some drowsiness for a day or so. It is often very welcome—enabling them to have a proper sleep for the first time for perhaps months. For elderly people, however, this initial drowsiness may be enough to allow pneumonia a foothold leading to death. It can be difficult to choose between relieving a patient's pain of perhaps weeks or months and *perhaps* hastening death. It is in fact quite likely that had appropriate analgesia been given to these patients before they reached such a debilitated state, they would be less likely to succumb to a chest infection, perhaps a little prematurely.

There is no clinical difference between diamorphine (heroin) and morphine (Twycross 1977). Diamorphine when made into a solution begins to degrade into morphine, and should usually be discarded if not used within six weeks because of the uncertainty of dosage. Morphine's shelf life would be similar, but degradation of both substances accelerates if they are combined in solution with, say, a phenothiazine. Under those circumstances they should be discarded within 2–3 weeks. These figures are approximate as work is continuing to try to determine them more accurately. However, as it is customary not to dispense more than is sufficient for 10–14 days, the problem of loss of potency should not arise. Diamorphine is approximately one third more potent than morphine. They are interchangeable in their use provided a simple dose adjustment is made (see Fig 5).

The other important calculation to remember is to halve the oral dose if intramuscular injections have to be given (see Fig 5). For injections diamorphine is preferable to morphine as it can be diluted in a minute quantity of water. The frequency of

oral morphine		oral diamorphine/ methadone		intramuscular diamorphine/ methadone
15 mg	equivalent to	10 mg	equivalent to	5 mg
30 mg	equivalent to	20 mg	equivalent to	10 mg
45 mg	equivalent to	30 mg	equivalent to	15 mg
60 mg	equivalent to	40 mg	equivalent to	20 mg

Fig 5

intramuscular diamorphine can be reduced to 6-hourly. Methadone is given by injection at 8-hourly intervals.

In England and around the world a profusion of opiate analgesic mixtures has developed. For example, 'Mist E' (E for euphoria), SAM (strong analgesic mixture), Mist Victoria Park (London Chest Hospital). In the United States of America there is a propensity for 'Hospice Mix'. All these recipes were derived from the 'Brompton Cocktail' a mixture concocted about 50 years ago for patients in the Brompton Hospital, London, following chest surgery—it no longer has a part to play in the care of dying patients.

Every patient's pain is different and every patient needs a dose of analgesic individually titrated specifically to relieve his pain. The Brompton mixture usually contained an inadequate dose of morphine or diamorphine. The euphoriant present was cocaine 5 mg and sometimes patients became needlessly sleepy by the 25 mg chlorpromazine (Largactil) it contained. Cocaine has been shown to serve no useful function in this context (Twycross 1979), and chlorpromazine may occasionally be used but only as major tranquilizer for very anxious patients.

Adjustments are made to the dose as necessary, initially perhaps several times in the first day or two, in order to achieve maximum analgesia: 10–20 mg morphine 4-hourly depending on the patient's previous analgesia and the severity of the pain, will be the usual starting dose. A 50% daily increase is often appropriate initially. However, some patients may need 150 mg morphine or more 4-hourly and in the higher dose ranges the increments would obviously be smaller.

A proportion of patients are nauseated by strong analgesics and it is wise to prescribe a routine antiemetic at least for the first week or so. One single bout of vomiting in a weak patient is an unnecessary addition to his suffering and might be enough to alienate him from his analgesia. Various antiemetics are in vogue, but prochlorperazine (Stemetil) 5 mg 4-hourly, either in the mixture or separately, has a record of reliability. Metoclopramide (Maxolon) 5 mg may also be added to the mixture if necessary.

The mixtures are most conveniently made up to a 5 or 10 ml dose. Another vital ingredient is the flavour. Morphine has an extremely bitter taste which can linger in the mouth. To encourage the patient to take it regularly for the rest of his life it would be wise and kind to make it palatable. Whisky, brandy, gin or fruit flavourings may be used (about 100 ml alcohol per 500 ml bottle). *Ask the patient* which he would prefer and include the flavouring as a routine part of the prescription. A small tot of brandy in a medicine can make for punctual and reliable time-keeping!

Punctuality is of course important. Oral morphine begins to take effect after about 30 minutes. It will then maintain that effect for approximately 4 hours. After 5–6 hours the patient will again experience pain. That is why it is so important to give the next dose before the effect of the previous one has worn off. '6-hourly prn' analgesia is useless for patients with pain from carcinomatosis. I have no experience of using such medication intravenously, but understand that toxic levels are more likely to be reached. In contrast, even if several hundred milligrams of morphine were taken accidentally by mouth by a patient already on a much lower dose mixture, it is unlikely he would come to any harm.

Some patients, especially if taking night sedation, may be pain-free on 5 doses of mixture a day. However, if the patient wakes with pain in the morning he should be advised to prepare a dose before retiring for the night, set the alarm for the appropriate hour, wake up, take the mixture and turn over and go back to sleep again. It is also important to remind him that if he is going out for the day or has a hospital appointment, then he should take with him a dose or doses in a small bottle, so that he does not risk the pain returning. The nurse should plan with the patient the times he will be taking the medicine, so that they fit in with the pattern of the household. Some families rise and go to bed early others get up late and go to bed late. Whatever is decided should then be adhered to fairly strictly.

Morphine suppositories are also available and can be most useful as they can be obtained in strengths from 5–200 mg. They are equivalent to an oral morphine dose and likewise should be administered 4-hourly. Their main use is when oxycodone suppositories are not appropriate—if a very low or very high level of analgesia is needed.

Current Trends in Analgesia

MST (a controlled drug) is a relatively new slow-release morphine tablet which is available in four strengths. Its great advantage is that it is designed to last for 12 hours (Clark 1982). The patient must be warned NOT TO CHEW OR CRUSH THE TABLETS. If he cannot swallow them he will need alternative medication. It is important to remember that the morphine dose of an MST tablet relates to 12 hours not 4 hours (see Fig 6). Some workers now claim it has an oral potency equivalent to diamorphine rather than to morphine (Tempest 1982). The patient's response to the analgesia will, as usual, be the best guide to the precise dose required:

MST Continus 12-hourly	10 mg	30 mg	60 mg	100 mg
Colour of tablet	buff	purple	peach	grey
Equivalent 4-hourly oral morphine dose	5 mg	15 mg	30 mg	50 mg
Equivalent 4-hourly oral diamorphine dose	3.3 mg	10 mg	20 mg	33.3 mg

Fig 6

Should the patient experience breakthrough pain before the 12 hours have elapsed, it is advisable to try the MST 8-hourly, particularly when using the larger doses. Alternatively, the dose may be increased by increasing the number of tablets given at 12-hourly intervals. The only disadvantage of these tablets is that unlike a mixture, it is not possible to increase the dose by 50%, unless the patient is supplied with different strength tablets. This is particularly important when using the 60 mg and 100 mg tablets.

Again it would be prudent to give the patient prophylactic antiemetics — 12 or 8-hourly may suffice, but 4-hourly may be necessary. The patient, unless very unreliable, can usually adjust or eliminate his antiemetic as he feels appropriate.

Adjuvant Pain Therapies

Radiotherapy can produce the most amazing results in many patients, some tumours being more responsive than others.

Mrs H. with myelomatosis and carcinomatosis from the bronchus suddenly became unable to weight-bear on her right leg while out shopping. The pain was so intense that she had difficulty in finding any comfortable position and even in bed she was virtually immobile. A portable X-ray showed no evidence of a pathological fracture. Rapid referral back to the local radiotherapy department for some treatment to the hip, enabled her within a short time to discard the walking frame and, eventually, the walking stick. Mrs H. showed a similar response as we raced to keep ahead of her painful tumour by irradiating her chest in two different places. Her morphine dose thus remained for most of the time at 20 mg 4-hourly during the two years we knew Mrs H. The dose was raised as a new problem presented and lowered again after the problem responded to radiotherapy.

However, some patients requiring a long course of radiotherapy can suffer enormously. While the actual treatment may only take a few minutes, the patient can be left sitting for hours waiting for transport, so that he arrives home utterly exhausted. This may occur two or three times a week for several weeks. Fortunately, many radiotherapists are becoming aware of this problem and try to amend their programmes to suit the patient's needs. Thus where purely symptomatic relief and not curative treatment is the aim, it may be possible to give a *single* treatment, rather than several, to an area such as a painful metastasis in a long bone. They are also beginning to realize that even if a metastasis does not show up on X-ray, it is often worth giving a single dose of irradiation to the area anyway.

One of the most distressing events which can occur when caring for a dying patient is if he should die during or just after completing a long and gruelling course of radiotherapy or chemotherapy. As nurses, we must have the courage of our convictions and communicate our fears to the radiotherapy department or general practitioner if such an occurrence seems likely. Decisions about whether or not to continue with treatment are often difficult to make but we have a duty to our patient to see that such matters are considered by the medical staff whenever there is a query. We cannot claim to be caring for a patient if we do not ask such questions when they seem appropriate.

Another way to minimize disruption of the patient's life is by an informal telephone approach to the radiotherapist, usually by the general practitioner. Some patients' metastases are unlikely to respond to radiotherapy and prior enquiry could save an unnecessary trip by the patient merely to be told that he could not be helped by such treatment.

Nerve blocks seem to produce a widely varying response (Mushin *et al.* 1977), although a skillful and enthusiastic anaesthetist may work wonders. Mrs D. on 25 mg morphine 4-hourly was totally pain-free following a nerve block to her chest wall. We reduced and finally discontinued her analgesia and eventually this lady was discharged from our care. Several years later she is still alive and well with her slowly metastasizing carcinoma of the breast. This lady had been confined to bed for some months before and after we first met her, but she eventually became ambulant.

Another patient with chest pain from his bronchial carcinoma and free-draining empyaema cavity experienced extreme discomfort and no relief from his nerve block. Usually an intercostal block can be performed with a minimum of discomfort and is often very effective.

Lumbar and sacral blocks may be useful, but possible faecal and urinary incontinence or impairment of function must be considered if a large part of the area needs blocking (Robbie 1969). Mr R. had intense and unremitting shooting sciatic pain only partly relieved by 100 mg morphine 4-hourly and anti-inflammatory medication. He already had a colostomy for his colonic carcinoma and an indwelling catheter for urinary retention. His pain was, he said, rendered 'liveable with' following two sacral blocks. A marked improvement in his mobility and interest in life was apparent.

Surgery can play an important part in the symptomatic relief of pain. The pinning of a pathological fracture with rapid mobilization and discharge of the patient back to the care of the community staff can be most effective. It sometimes helps to pin a bone if it appears likely to fracture, in order to relieve the pain. Surgical intervention is well illustrated by Mrs P. who, following radical mastectomy, had a grossly lymphoedematous right arm which was in a permanently flexed position. The arm caused constant pain and discomfort and was an unhealthy purple colour by the time we met her several years postoperatively. During the previous two years she had requested amputation of the arm on several occasions, and been refused. However, it seemed reasonable that, as she was likely to require daily dressings for her radiotherapy necrosis and tumour, that process could be facilitated by resection of the necrotic area and arm, leaving a relatively clean stump area to be dressed instead. A venturesome surgeon, who understands the needs of dying patients, following a domiciliary visit to the patient, agreed to operate. Her remaining six months of life were transformed as she became mobile once more and able to go out with help. Incidentally, the wound surprised us by almost healing in that time.

A transcutaneous nerve stimulator (TNS or TENS) may be helpful for some patients' pain. It appears more effective when the cause is other than malignancy.

Acupuncture and acupressure are proving to be most effective in some areas of pain relief. The development of TNS and surge of interest in acupuncture are partly the result of the advances in the understanding of the physiology of pain.

Relaxation, meditation, auto-hypnosis, imagery and visualization are techniques being enthusiastically practised on the west coast of America, and to a lesser extent in the UK (Woolley-Hart 1979). Any non-injurious method of improving a patient's pain relief is worth considering, but training and skill in the use of these therapies would be needed. The availability of people with adequate time and training currently restricts the widespread adoption of these approaches (Hoy 1977).

Entonox (nitrous oxide and oxygen) is sometimes useful (Zorab 1978) — particularly when carrying out painful dressings or other techniques. From my experience, a local midwifery unit will probably loan the equipment for a trial period or for a particular patient with a short prognosis.

Ice massage to a painful area may also bring some relief.

If it is difficult to achieve effective pain relief, or to acquire equipment such as TNS, referring the patient to a pain clinic may provide the solution (Swerdlow 1978). Pain clinics are usually run by experienced anaesthetists, and The Intractable Pain Society (Appendix 2) can supply a list of addresses. The main disadvantage is that it may take several weeks to obtain an appointment. About 15–30% of their patients have a neoplasm. Referral is, of course, by the general practitioner.

Further discussion of the most appropriate treatment for specific pain is included in Chapter 3.

Chapter 3

Management of Symptoms and Common Problems

Say thank you, God,
If you're free of pain,
If someone needs help,
Don't turn away.
ER (A patient)

Today we do not need to turn away from our patients who need help. Today we have no excuse for saying 'there is nothing more we can do for you'. Today and for many days in the past 30 years or so heroic efforts have been made in order to offer therapeutic as well as loving care to someone close to death. Perhaps the best development has been the gradual realization by medical staff that patients do die and that there does come a point in the progress of the disease where aggressive curative treatment is no longer appropriate. What then becomes important is the maximum physical and mental relief from any distressing symptoms however minor they may appear to the onlooker. This then frees the patient to prepare for death if and how he so wishes — be it prayer or pub (or both!)

The list of problems or symptoms that patients may experience is long but, as in so many areas of life, some patients seem to develop one problem after another, while others may have very few.

Although the symptoms described are found in patients with carcinomatosis, many of them would also be present with other terminal illnesses. If there are situations or symptoms not discussed here which prove obstinate, it is hoped that the reader will rise to the challenge and work with the members of the primary care team to find a solution.

39

Accurate assessment of each symptom is the basis for symptomatic treatment. However, it is often appropriate to institute a trial of therapy while awaiting the results of tests. Thus, if it is likely that a steroid would help—start it straight away. The clinical response will often precede and obviate the result from the laboratory. If the treatment after a few days is not working as hoped then it can be discontinued or amended as necessary. Empirical treatment for a symptom must be given even if its cause cannot be ascertained or deduced.

The following list of symptoms and conditions is arranged in approximate order of frequency with which they were met in the Macmillan Service during the years 1979 and 1980. This may give some indication of the likely frequency with which community staff will encounter similar problems.

Bone pain may be partially helped by strong analgesics such as morphine, but for some time now it has been known that drugs with an anti-inflammatory action may often be more helpful (Twycross 1978c). It is believed that such drugs inhibit the production of some prostaglandins. Prostaglandins, it is thought, increase the individual's awareness of pain—probably by sensitization of nerve endings. Thus benorylate (Benoral), aspirin, indomethacin (Indocid), phenyl-butazone (Butazolidin) or diflunisal (Dolobid) may be effective with or without morphine. If the aspirin-like drugs cause unacceptable side effects (indigestion, sweating, etc) then zomepirac (Zomax), which is also a prostaglandin inhibitor (Lancet 1976), may be a useful substitute. A steroid such as 2–4 mg dexamethesone daily could be tried as an alternative.

If the pain can be localized to a particular tender spot—such as the neck of the femur or a rib—then a single dose of radiotherapy may eliminate the need for medication. Surgical intervention may be indicated if the bone is painful and likely to fracture.

Abdominal visceral pain commonly results from stretching of the liver capsule. It may be treated with morphine if unrelieved by milder analgesics. If the pain is unremitting a coeliac or intrathecal nerve block should be considered. A further course of radiotherapy, perhaps to bladder or uterine tumours, may relieve pain. Colic is distinguished from other abdominal pain by its intermittent nature: the likeliest cause is constipation. If it is the result of obstruction by a tumour, propantheline (Pro-banthine) 8-hourly may help (see intestinal obstruction).

Nerve compression may be relieved or paraplegia prevented by giving radiotherapy to a collapsing vertebra. Appropriate analgesics may also be required with perhaps a trial of steroids. A nerve block may be effective if other methods fail.

Raised intracranial pressure usually presents with a combination of nausea, vomiting, dizziness, diplopia, blurred vision and headache. Such symptoms are often indicative of cerebral metastases. Another presentation may be with an acute onset of fits.

A course of radiotherapy could be considered if the patient is well enough, but the usual treatment in the latter stages of the disease is with steroids. Dexamethasone 6–16 mg daily is usually required initially. It is thought that the steroid acts on the cerebral oedema—not on the tumour which will continue to grow. As the symptoms subside the steroid dose is reduced to the lowest possible level consistent with keeping the symptoms controlled. The addition of a diuretic rather than an increase of dexamethasone may be helpful. The medication is continued until the symptoms of raised intracranial pressure begin to recur. The dose is then lowered rapidly and the patient allowed to lapse into coma and die peacefully.

Although many patients can be astonishingly improved by such treatment, it may be helpful to have a team discussion before prescribing steroids for cerebral metastases. The side effects of high dosage are so distressing, and partly successful treatment may simply prolong a sorrowful situation for the patient; therefore, they should not be used without careful consideration. Similarly, increasing the dose every time symptoms recur is an inept response which lays up more problems for the family later. It can be likened to adding oil to a fire which is already out of control.

Constipation. If a patient presents with any combination of:

anorexia
nausea
vomiting
colicky abdominal pain
urinary retention
abdominal distention
borborygmi
diarrhoea

} before you let a doctor concoct more ingenious diagnoses—think BOWELS!

Visitors to the Macmillan Service initially believe that its staff are possessed by some sort of bowel fixation. However, the guest is rapidly enlightened, when accompanying the doctor to see new patients, as he is confronted by constipation in approximately one third of those patients. The story is frequently that the patient has had no bowel action for two or three weeks—or longer. Relatives, and too many professionals, are heard to say 'Well, he's not eating much so he won't have his bowels open very often will he?' For most people a daily bowel action is normal. When the appetite is severely impaired the body's waste products, and over thirty feet of intestine, will manufacture enough faeces for a bowel action every three to four days, even just prior to death.

Mrs S., with a colostomy, was referred with 'only days to live', because of vomiting and dehydration due to a supposed bowel obstruction. Within two weeks, and following several enemas, that lady was watching the Royal Ballet at Covent Garden, sitting next to the Royal Box. She was accompanied by a nurse with a vomit bowl—just in case! After the performance the principal dancers presented her with their flowers. Mrs S. lived another six months.

The onset of constipation will occur directly with the majority of analgesics—even in low dosage. To counteract it a stool softener and sometimes a stimulant is required. In this country Dorbanex suspension, capsules or Forte (danthron + poloxamer '188') are probably the most useful. The patient *must* be warned in advance that Dorbanex colours the urine red, lest he be worried that he has haematuria. Dorbanex *Forte* is usually needed for any patient on morphine or equivalent. It is more than three times as potent as the suspension or capsules. Divided doses of 5–40 ml daily may be required—depending on the stamina and taste buds of the patient. Some like it, some loathe it, and some develop a rash on the buttocks and legs when they take it. A patient in the two latter categories may be managed with a combination of lactulose (Duphalac) or Dioctyl Forte (dioctyl sodium sulphosuccinate) tablets, with senna (Sennokot) as a stimulant. Some hospices find that liberal doses of senna extract—especially as senna tea—are effective without adjuvant softeners. The appropriate doses have to be established for each patient, but 60 ml of lactulose or 6 tablets of Dioctyl Forte, may be required daily.

If the rectum is full of faeces, or while waiting for the oral medication to take effect, which may be 3–4 days, Dulcolax (bisacodyl) suppositories should be given. In fact even if the rectum is empty, suppositories may still be usefully given if constipation is suspected. Whenever a rectal examination is performed or suppositories are inserted it is essential to watch the patient's face: this will usually ensure the procedure is carried out as gently as possible.

An enema is, in my view, usually unnecessary. It increases the suffering of a weak and sick patient, who probably would be unable to retain the fluid long enough to reach even a commode, or in sufficient quantity for it to be effective. Manual removal of faeces (Chapter 4) may occasionally need to be performed.

The patient should be told that aperients may take several days to produce a result. If this is not explained he will probably expect a bowel action the following day. Should this not occur he may either discard the medication as useless or take excessive doses which may produce a catastrophic result as he struggles to reach the toilet or commode in a great hurry. This book is written from bitter experience!

Anorexia is commonly caused by constipation, nausea and vomiting, hypercalcaemia, fatigue, anxiety or depression, badly prepared food, a bad taste in the mouth or a dry or sore mouth, and is a troublesome symptom for many patients.

When so many other activities are becoming curtailed, loss of appetite may seem like the last straw. Hypercalcaemia (Twycross 1972) is a fairly common cause and occurs especially when a patient has bony metastases. Dexamethasone 2 mg daily will usually correct it, as evidenced by a clinical improvement within a few days. After a week or so the dose may be halved to 1 mg and then to 0.5 mg tablets as a long-term maintenance dose—or whichever dose keeps the symptoms abated. As steroids have a systemic mode of action it is questionable whether the more expensive enteric-coated prednisolone would prevent gastric irritation. Using dexamethasone also reduces the number of tablets the patient has to swallow (dexamethasone 1 mg is equivalent to 7 mg prednisolone). It is important to try to ensure that the pharmacist does not supply 0.5 mg tablets when the patient is on a higher dose of dexamethasone, or he may end up taking handfuls of them each day. A 2 mg tablet is available—the pharmacist should order them if necessary.

Sometimes the unpleasant taste which flavours all food and drink can be relieved by giving zinc supplements such as Zincomed 8-hourly.

Dyspnoea is most frequently caused by tumours intrinsic and extrinsic to the bronchi, superior mediastinal masses pressing on the trachea or chronic obstructive airways disease. Pleural effusion or thickening, congestive cardiac failure or infection may also provoke dyspnoea.

This symptom is generally more difficult to treat and vastly more distressing for the patient than pain. Oxygen (unless the patient is already used to it) is of little value for the majority of these patients, who may even feel worse because of the suffocating effect if a face-mask is used. Chest aspiration occasionally helps if there is an effusion, but again may cause more distress than it relieves if the procedure is performed insensitively. Should the patient feel little or no benefit from one chest aspiration, he is unlikely to benefit from further attempts. *Ask the patient.* Congestive cardiac failure should be treated in the usual way.

Careful consideration is needed when prescribing antibiotics. The majority of patients will die peacefully from a chest infection. Antibiotics should not be given if they will not improve the health of the patient but merely prolong his dying. However, if the chest infection produces a distressing degree of dyspnoea then an antibiotic can be administered to relieve such symptoms. Once or twice daily medication such as Vibramycin, Tetrabid (tetracyclines) or Septrin (trimethoprim) is much more tolerable for the patient, who by this time will be very weak.

If he is not already having an opiate, a small dose of morphine 5-10 mg + prochlorperazine 5 mg 4-hourly as a mixture, may be helpful. The respiratory depression side effect of morphine, feared by so many, is thus turned to good effect. In fact this side effect is overemphasized, being dangerous only to patients with chronic respiratory disease: it can be safely ignored for most patients. A dyspnoeic patient may be helped by the reduction of the respiratory rate and the sensation of gasping for breath. The morphine dose may be adjusted as necessary.

Upper mediastinal tumours may cause, and can present fairly rapidly with, swelling of the neck and distension of jugular veins associated with acute dyspnoea and stridor. The veins may distend on the chest, and the face, arms and trunk become dusky-coloured. This is described as superior vena caval obstruction. It usually requires urgent treatment. Dexamethasone 12-16 mg daily in divided doses will usually dramatically improve the situation. If the patient is well enough, a course of radiotherapy would then be the treatment of choice, following which the steroids may be reduced or discontinued. Physiotherapy, relaxation and diversionary techniques and bronchodilators should be used where appropriate.

Cough which can prevent the patient from having adequate rest, may be non-productive or productive. A patient with a productive cough may or may not have difficulty with expectoration. This may be aided by bromhexine (Bisolvon) which liquifies sputum. If a bronchodilator is required it can be combined with orciprenaline as Alupent expectorant—it also tastes better than bromxhexine alone. Benylin expectorant, although it may taste nice, is an illogical medication as it contains a cough suppressant and expectorant—a very confusing 'message' for the body to receive.

Suppression of a non-productive cough may be achieved with linctus codeine 10 ml in hot water, or a small dose of methadone (Physeptone) linctus, or morphine 5-10 mg 4-hourly (if the patient is not already taking it as an analgesic). Physiotherapy and steam inhalations may aid expectoration. The combination of an expectorant by day and cough suppressant at night may be helpful for some patients.

A cough is occasionally a symptom of a tracheo-oesophageal fistula. Death from inhalational pneumonia will usually follow fairly quickly. The patient should if possible be offered the choice of being kept fairly sleepy in order to prevent physical distress.

If the patient is too weak to cough and begins to 'rattle', 8–12-hourly injections of hyoscine 0.4 mg or atropine 0.6 mg may be given. These injections should *not* usually be given to a patient who is still conscious because they further dry his mouth when he is probably dehydrated anyway. Probably the best course is to have a chat with the relatives (Chapter 7) who may be more distressed by it than the patient.

Anxiety will probably be experienced to a greater or lesser degree by most patients. Some may become mildly anxious on reaching such a significant point in their lives. Others have always been so anxious that with any new event or change of circumstance, however minor, that the advance of debilitating illness and the approach of death, fills them with a terror which is sad to behold.

The main treatment is listening, and honest discussion with the patient of the many causes of his anxiety. Should medication be necessary 2–5 mg diazepam (Valium) 8-hourly may help. Alternatively, if the patient is already taking a morphine mixture, a small dose of chlorpromazine (Largactil) 5–7.5 mg 4-hourly may be added. This can be increased, if the patient is severely anxious, to a dose just below that which would make him sleepy. Once the anxiety is relieved, it may be possible to lower the analgesic dose.

Depression, like anxiety, usually involves taking the time to listen to the patient or encourage him to talk. He may under-standably be depressed for many reasons, but if this is the result of boredom or inactivity it should be possible to find a remedy. Antidepressants may be needed, especially if the patient is sleeping badly. Trimipramine (Surmontil) 50–150 mg or mianserin (Bolvidon) 30–60 mg at night may be effective. The patient may need to be advised to take this several hours before bedtime — if he is troubled by drowsiness during the day.

Dry mouth is a problem for which everyone, whether doctor or nurse, is constantly seeking new methods of treatment (Lipman 1975). (There are many suggestions for treating the problem. I would be glad to hear from any reader who has a favourite remedy which may not be generally known about.) The most frequent cause is the use of strong analgesics and phenothiazines. The first remedy, therefore, is to keep the dose of such medications as low as possible and to review frequently all drug therapy with this in mind.

Obviously, adequate hydration — where possible — and good mouth care are important. Ice or pineapple chunks to suck, appeal to some patients. Chewing-gum may also stimulate the salivary glands. Occasionally fluid may be given rectally, if the patient is very distressed, but it is not usually required. Similarly, intravenous fluids and the restriction of movement which they entail, are rarely appropriate when a patient is dying — although a relatively fast infusion can be given in the patient's home. (I have seen this twice in 7 years and nearly 2,000 dying patients.)

A solution of 'artificial saliva' can be prepared by a local pharmacist. There are various recipes but 10 g methylcellulose per litre of water with some lemon flavouring, is about the simplest. The patient is instructed to take a teaspoonful of it as necessary.

Mouth swabs with lemon glycerine may be appreciated by some patients, but the sweet stickiness may not be liked by all.

Excessive salivation occurs occasionally and may be helped by tinct. belladonna or other atropine-like drug.

Sore mouth is usually caused by monilial infection (thrush), frequently seen in cachectic patients who are taking steroids and/or antibiotics. Nystatin oral suspension 1 ml 4-hourly, swilled around the mouth and swallowed, or miconazole

(Daktarin gel) 5–10 ml 4-hourly are usually rapidly effective and should be given for forty-eight hours after a clinical cure. If the patient has false teeth, these should be soaked overnight in the suspension. Thrush tends to recur and the mouth should be checked with a torch whenever the patient is visited. Occasionally it is necessary to resort to painting the mouth with gentian violet—a good old-fashioned remedy that never fails—although it may be a bit messy.

Nausea and vomiting may have many causes. These include: constipation, drugs, anxiety, hypercalcaemia, carcinomatosis from the ovary or stomach, radiotherapy, chemotherapy, uraemia, raised intracranial pressure, intestinal obstruction, infections or cough. Some of these conditions are described separately in this chapter.

As with other symptoms, it is important to establish a cause. This can usually be done by clinical acumen, and discovery of the cause should be followed rapidly by the initiation of some form of treatment. If there has been no satisfactory response within a few days the doctor may then consider investigation of serum calcium, urea and electrolytes. While awaiting the results treatment using alternative medication should be instituted. It is quite unjustifiable in these circumstances to allow the patient's suffering to continue while awaiting blood results which could well be mislaid in the laboratory or fed incorrectly into the computer.

Although opiates and other strong analgesics are often the cause of drug-induced nausea, at least initially, it is important to consider other likely possibilities such as digoxin, aspirin or benorylate, some antibiotics—particularly Vibramycin—cytotoxics and oestrogens.

Antiemetics fall into three main categories each having a different mode of action and therefore likely to be more or less appropriate in treating the different causes of nausea and vomiting.

Phenothiazines such as prochlorperazine (Stemetil), chlorpromazine (Largactil), methotrimiprazine (Nozinan) and promazine (Sparine) act on the chemoreceptor trigger zone in the medulla. Haloperidol (Serenace) has a similar action.

Patients with hypercalcaemia, uraemia or drug-induced nausea may be helped by these antiemetics. Prochlorperazine 5 mg 4-hourly has the advantage of being less sedating than the others — if sedation is not desired.

Antihistamines depress the vomiting centres. These include cyclizine (Valoid) and promethazine (Phenergan), and may be of particular benefit to patients with low bowel obstruction or ascites. Cyclizine 50 mg by mouth, or, more frequently by intramuscular injection, can be very helpful if the patient is exhausted from frequent or sudden onset of symptoms. It seems to provide a comforting rest and effectively arrests the vomiting. After treating the cause — such as constipation or infection, the cyclizine can often be discontinued or perhaps changed to prochlorperazine to prevent drowsiness.

Metoclopramide (Maxolon) 10 mg 8-hourly acts on the chemoreceptor trigger zone and also by increasing normal peristalsis and relaxing the pyloric sphincter. It can be given by mouth as a tablet or a syrup — the latter may be included in a morphine mixture or given as a 2 ml injection. It is particularly helpful with the symptoms of delayed gastric emptying, perhaps from carcinoma of the stomach or gross ascites.

Although antiemetics have a particular mode of action, it is recommended that if one does not prove effective another from a different group be tried. Some patients will respond to a combination of anti-emetics.

When making any changes in medication, particularly with antiemetics, it is important to make only one change at a time in order to determine which drug is effective.

Oedema can often be more mentally than physically upsetting for the patient. It may take the form of lymphoedema of limbs from mastectomy or pelvic obstruction of venous return caused by metastases or ascites. Ankle and leg oedema may result from hypoproteinaemia as the patient's nutritional and general condition deteriorates; or with the onset of circulatory failure. Occasionally massively enlarged scrotum and genitalia may occur.

The treatment of lymphoedema of the arm or leg may lie in the use of an intermittent compression pump. Jobst International

(17 Wigmore Street, London W1) have these for hire and provide instruction, but it may be possible to borrow one from a local hospital. Each health authority should have them available. The patient can be taught how to use the machine, which when set up is very simple, and often most effective.

Occasionally a large dose of dexamathasone 12–16 mg daily may reduce the oedema round a lower abdominal tumour, thereby aiding venous return. If there is no response in about four or five days it should be discontinued.

Diuretics may help if the oedema is the result of the cachectic condition of the patient. Amiloride + hydrochlorothiazide (Moduretic) is a convenient size to swallow, although frusemide (Lasix) may be appropriate on occasions.

Scrotal oedema from carcinoma of the prostate may respond dramatically to a large dose of stilboestrol. Oedema from thrombosis in deep veins should be managed in the usual way.

Discharge may be from any orifice and can be a source of great embarrassment to the patient, particularly if it is smelly. A swab for culture of the organisms should be taken and appropriate antibiotic given. A course of metronidazole (Flagyl) can be wonderfully effective, bringing rapid relief to patients with carcinoma of the breast, cervix or uterus. It should be commenced as soon as swabs have been taken, without waiting for the results.

Insomnia may be physically or mentally induced. Physical problems such as cough, dyspnoea or pain should be treated and may be easier to cure than the mental reasons for insomnia, which must be discussed with the patient even if night sedation is also required. Fear of perhaps not waking up or anxiety about relatives or business affairs may not unnaturally produce insomnia. Should sedation be necessary a short-acting benzo-diazepine may be given. Temazepam (Euhypnos, Normison) 10–30 mg or diazepam (Valium) 5–10 mg are easier to swallow and produce less of a hangover the following day than nitrazepam (Mogadon), with its much longer half-life. Occasionally a barbiturate may be required if other hypnotics fail.

Dysphagia can be tormenting for a patient if he has to watch his family work their way through a plate of fish and chips knowing that he cannot. The most likely cause is from monilial infection (see sore mouth). However, dysphagia may also be a temporary or permanent response to radiotherapy or be caused by mechanical blockage by tumour either in or outside the lumen of the oesophagus.

Insertion of an oesophageal tube—such as Mousseau Barbin —may be possible if the patient is fit enough. If it becomes blocked by food (especially green salad), fizzy drinks may release the obstruction. Local anaesthetic mixtures such as Mucaine may aid swallowing. Advice should be given on diet and liquidization of food. If fluids cannot be swallowed death will occur within a short time and the patient must be kept comfortable and free from distressing symptoms—he may prefer to be kept fairly sleepy at this point in order not to experience the discomfort of dehydration.

Prolonging dying by performing a gastrostomy at this time is unjustifiable and will usually mean an unpleasant death for the patient. The tube may drop out as gastric secretions burn his abdominal wall, and as the tumour grows it will put pressure on structures like the trachea, with the consequence of suffocation —a most undesirable manner in which to die.

Urinary tract problems usually take the form of retention, incontinence or infection. Retention may be a consequence of impairment of the nerve supply by compression, nerve block, cerebral tumour or approaching death. It may result from blockage of the urethra from external compression in a constipated patient (the commonest cause), tumour or ascites, or as a side effect of anticholinergic medication such as propantheline (Pro-banthine). Indwelling catheterization may be required if the condition cannot be relieved, and should be performed prophylactically when imminent mechanical blockage is likely.

Incontinence, feared by many as they become weaker, should be avoided. Because, as nurses, we do not mind coping with a wet bed it is easy to forget, or not even to realize, how it feels to the patient. Management may be more difficult if there is a vesico-vaginal or recto-vesical fistula. Catheterization may help —and should usually be performed for incontinence in the few days prior to death. By the time they died 27% of the patients in the care of the Macmillan Service had been catheterized.

Frequency or incontinence at night may be eliminated by emepronium bromide (Cetiprin) 200 mg, which relaxes the bladder. The patient's drinking habits should be monitored and he should be advised not to take much fluid in the evening.

Urinary infection which gives rise to troublesome symptoms should always be treated with an antibiotic—even if the patient has only a short time to live.

Indigestion, like dysphagia, can discourage eating—perhaps one of the few pleasures left for a very ill patient. It is commonly a side effect of medication with steroids or other anti-inflammatory agent. It is vitally important to review such medication frequently, aiming to keep the dose as low as possible. Cimetidine (Tagamet) may need to be given if the symptoms are severe and not responding to antacids. Mucaine— which contains a local anaesthetic as well as aluminium hydroxide can be helpful if taken about 10 minutes before food or drink. It is worth remembering that aluminium hydroxide is constipating and magnesium salts may bring on diarrhoea.

Waterbrash, experienced by some patients with carcinoma of the stomach or oesophagus, is regurgitation of mouthfuls of saliva-like secretions. Some patients experience relief from a teaspoon-ful of clear (runny) honey following any food or drink. As it is such a simple remedy it is always worth trying. It is also an easy and nourishing way of increasing carbohydrate intake.

Ascites should be relieved by abdominal paracentesis if it is causing the patient discomfort. This can be performed very simply at home by an enterprising general practitioner and saves the patient much of the distress and trauma associated with a hospital admission for such a relatively minor procedure. The main effort involved is in acquiring a peritoneal dialysis cannula from a friend in a local hospital. Paracentesis can then be carried out at home using a local anaesthetic and draining the ascitic fluid into a handy receptacle such as a bucket. The risk of cross-infection at home is negligible and the Macmillan Service has never encountered such a problem, having employed the procedure on numerous occasions. It usually takes about an hour and it has never appeared necessary to drain the abdomen slowly in order to avoid shock. A small black silk suture may be removed 3–4 days later. The relief of the patient at not having to go into hospital at regular intervals is so great that, once they have tried it, most general practitioners would probably be happy to continue with such treatment.

Pleural effusion can similarly be treated at home by chest aspiration. However, many patients find chest aspiration to be an uncomfortable procedure if it is not carried out with great care. If it does not relieve the symptoms to any degree the patient should not be subjected to repeat performances. (In 1979, of 334 patients with carcinomatosis being attended at home by the Macmillan Service, 14 paracenteses and 4 chest aspirations were performed.)

Sweating may occur, particularly at night, and appears to be associated with liver and lung metastases. Some patients experience complete relief from the use of an indomethacin (Indocid) 100 mg suppository at night.

Hiccoughs, if persistent, will rapidly exhaust the patient. The most usual causes are uraemia, phrenic nerve disturbance or irritation of the diaphragm by tumour. Traditional methods of treatment such as breathing into a paper bag may be tried. Mucaine may help. The medications most likely to be effective are metoclopramide (Maxolon) 10 mg 8-hourly or chlorpromazine (Largactil) 25–50 mg 6-hourly or when necessary.

Drowsiness may be particularly annoying for a patient who is struggling to remain active either physically, mentally or both. On the other hand it may be a welcome state for a patient who is weak, cachectic and approaching death. Treatment should therefore be appropriate to the patient's general state of health, the progress of his disease—and his wishes.

Drowsiness may be relieved by changing or stopping night sedation or advising the patient to take it a few hours earlier in the evening. If it is a symptom of newly-diagnosed raised intracranial pressure it may be treated as described earlier in the chapter. If it occurs following such treatment then it is perhaps time to consider tailing off the medication to allow nature to take its course. The same applies if drowsiness is caused by uraemia or a chest infection in a very weak patient.

A few patients find that the strong, narcotic analgesics cause drowsiness. Some can tolerate a high dose with no problems and others may keep falling asleep on a relatively low dose. These latter patients may be helped remarkably by dextamphetamine sulphate (Dexedrine) 5 mg once or twice during the early part of the day—say, at 7 am and 11 am. It should not be given later in case it prevents proper sleep at night. This treatment sometimes reduces the appetite, which may already be diminished, and if this does happen the best course would be to discuss his preferences with the patient.

Diarrhoea, unlike the majority of problems, may occasionally be difficult to relieve at home and necessitate admission to hospital because the care giver has become exhausted. The first line of thought must be whether the patient has had too much aperient, or not enough—the latter case producing spurious diarrhoea from a faecal impaction (Wilkes 1981). A rectal examination will usually clarify the situation.

Some patients may have diarrhoea from taking antibiotics. Before deciding on the cause it is wise to check if the patient has eaten anything recently, such as cold pork pie, which may have sparked off the episode.

Insufficiency of pancreatic enzymes resulting from tumour may leave the patient with bulky, offensive stools which float (in the toilet). Replacement of the enzymes by Pancrex V, with food, may ameliorate the condition. The capsule has to be opened and its contents sprinkled on the food.

Diarrhoea from other causes may be effectively treated with loperamide (Imodium) 2–4 mg up to 6-hourly, or one capsule after every loose bowel action.

Fits are usually related to a cerebral tumour. If they occur in spite of radiotherapy and steroids, phenytoin (Epanutin) 300 mg daily may be given. Phenobarbitone 30–60 mg 8 or 12-hourly may also be required. Sufficient medication/sedation should be given to control the symptoms, which if severe, will probably indicate that the patient has not long to live. Phenobarbitone 60–200 mg 8-hourly by injection may become necessary.

Itching is commonly caused by obstructive jaundice. Before assuming that this is the cause, the possibility of a reaction to medication — such as chlorpromazine — should be considered. It may even be due to scabies. Surgical procedures may relieve the jaundice and irritation temporarily. If it returns the patient may be helped by cholestyramine. The most palatable form available at present is Questran, 4 g per sachet. One sachet dissolved in a glass of fluid twice daily is the usual dose. It may take several days before the irritation is relieved.

Intestinal obstruction generally presents as a partial obstruction which may occur at intervals over several months prior to the final episode. It has been surprising how intermittent these occurrences can be — several patients living much longer than expected. The symptoms are usually of severe intermittent abdominal pain (colic), nausea and vomiting. It is essential to rule out constipation as the cause of the obstruction; misdiagnosis can, and probably does cost the life of some patients.

Subacute obstruction can be contained initially with stool softeners such as lactulose (Duphalac), combined with propantheline (Pro-banthine) 15 mg tablet 8-hourly, diphenoxylate + atropine (Lomotil) 1–2 tablets 6–8 hourly, or loperamide hydrochloride (Imodium) 1 capsule 6–8-hourly, for the colic. Frequently the medication can be tolerated by mouth, but if not the antiemetic may be given by suppository 6–8-hourly. The rectal dose of prochlorperazine is 25 mg, chlorpromazine 100 mg and cyclizine 50 mg. Metoclopramide (Maxolon) is contraindicated because it would exacerbate the colic.

Using a combination of antiemetics may relieve the nausea more effectively than one drug alone, and enable the patient to take some food. He may vomit sometime later, but with relatively little effort and without nausea—more like a regurgitation—and is then more able to tolerate the situation.

When the patient's condition deteriorates, the stool softener should be discontinued.

Confusion occurring in the last day or so of life is discussed on pp.77–78. If it presents at an earlier stage in the illness the cause should be established and appropriately treated. Confusion may be due to primary or secondary cerebral tumour and would perhaps respond to radiotherapy and/or steroids.

It is often forgotten that medication, including pentazocine (Fortral) and perphenazine (Fentazin), may produce confusion and hallucinations in some patients. Other precipitating factors include biochemical changes from uraemia, hypoglycaemia or infection of the lung or urine. Some elderly patients, even in their own homes, may have a reversal of sleep pattern, turning night into day, which may make them confused. Coping with this may depend on whether the care givers can to some extent reverse their sleep pattern also.

Haemorrhage is perhaps the best illustration of the difference between attitudes required in the care of people who are dying, and those who are not. Professional training has instilled in us the need for spontaneous action to arrest any degree of bleeding. When faced with a patient who is spurting blood from an artery eroded by tumour what is to be done? Instinct says apply pressure to the bleeding point. However, such action is futile, unlike the little boy who put his finger in the dyke to keep out the water. Even if we can stop the flow it would continue as soon as the pressure was released. A large arterial bleed will usually mean rapid death for the patient. If a nurse or doctor is present the only course of action is to have a dark-coloured towel or blanket available to wrap around the patient and soak up the blood, and then to stay very close to that patient as comfortably and peacefully as possible. If there is time and the means are available, intramuscular sedation (or intravenous if a doctor is present) may be given, but it is secondary to *remaining with the patient*.

Should the patient have a haemoptysis which does not prove fatal, further bleeding may be prevented by a course of radiotherapy, which may temporarily exacerbate the condition.

Intermittent haematemesis may justify the administration of cimetidine (Tagamet) to control symptoms if they are caused by peptic ulceration—perhaps from steroids.

Bleeding from the vagina or urinary tract will usually take place over a longer period and treatment, if any, should be symptomatic. Ethamsylate (Dicynene) 500 mg 6-hourly can inhibit oozing haemorrhages.

Blood transfusion is very rarely indicated at such a late stage in the illness, unless there are special circumstances such as an imminent family event for which the patient is struggling to stay alive.

Oxidized cellulose (Oxycel) is an impregnated gauze dressing which may stop slow venous bleeding, for example of a fungating breast. It is only available in hospital, which is regrettable, because it means that community nurses can only obtain it by subterfuge.

Muscle spasm may result from nocturnal cramp, and is often helped by quinine bisulphate 300 mg at night. Diazepam (Valium) 2–5 mg 8-hourly may also relieve symptoms. For muscle spasticity baclophen (Lioresal) 40–60 mg daily is valuable.

The treatments described in this chapter have evolved mainly in the past 15–20 years. This evolution is continuous, as the search to provide more effective ways of helping our patients carries on.

Chapter 4

Other Aspects of Nursing Care

It doesn't cost a penny,
That tender touch or word,
Go ahead and try it,
And you will feel superb.

ER (A patient)

'Nurse' derives from a word that means to nourish. Remembering this would perhaps ensure that fuller attention is given to the needs of the patient, and full attention should result in more effective organization of work, with appropriate nourishment as the outcome.

Fortunately, many nurses are alert to the special needs of dying people. Far from allowing any resting on laurels, this awareness stimulates the desire for continuous refinement of the nursing art. The closer a person is to death, the more basic and less technical become his nursing requirements. The more basic they become, the more skilfully they need to be executed.

Perhaps all nurses should have the opportunity to be a patient. We are always the 'doers'—rarely are we able to experience the pleasant, (and not so pleasant sensations) of being 'done to'. Were we more often patients, it is likely that the increasing habit of wearing rings and wrist-watches when carrying out nursing care, would quickly be dropped. We would appreciate the chill feeling of damp skin exposed to the air, or the sensation of talcum powder extravagantly applied to an incompletely dried area. We should also be aware of how distressing it can be for the patient, every time his bed is knocked. Nursing care, especially when it involves moving the patient, must be carried out slowly and deliberately avoiding excessive movements which tire, and add to his discomfort.

A patient's sense of smell might mean he would prefer a sore bottom rather than being moved around the bed by a nurse who had smoked a cigarette before entering his home, and was consequently breathing stale nicotine all over him.

A dying patient may need little physical care from the nurse until, perhaps, a day or so prior to death. As the needs increase, it is essential to be aware of the feeling of frustration and loss of dignity that he may experience. The body is taken for granted by most of us until it stops responding to familiar commands such as 'do the washing up' or 'dig the garden'. When this lack of response occurs it is often difficult to adjust to the situation and frequently the nurse knows (quite rightly) that the patient needs, for example, a commode, but the patient is not yet ready to accept his need. We must move at his pace, even if, in our opinion, he will suffer more. All care should involve maintenance of the dignity of the patient — and independence for as long as he wants it.

Washing the Patient

Great skill is necessary to wash a sick, weak patient so that he is left comfortable, satisfied and contented. It is one of the greatest services we can render to a patient.

Again, consideration of the senses is vital. What is 'touch' like to the patient? Many would probably rather not be washed if it means a bowl of tepid water with a bar of soap sloshing around at the bottom, resulting in an uncomfortable feeling on the skin as the soapy water is dried off with the towel.

Little intervention from the nurse may be required until the late stages of the illness. A wife caring for her husband will usually, if able, want to perform this important task, although she may need some instruction. It is vital to recognize when a spouse can manage and when she is 'soldiering on' because she doesn't like to ask for help. The need for help usually arises when the patient is unable to move himself without assistance. As busy nurses we can be tempted not to notice that help is required.

Some patients need and want to be washed all over every day, but others will allow the intrusion of soap and water with reluctance, and considerably less frequently. Attempting to change such basic and personal habits might well put at risk the efforts of the nurse to build a trusting and confident relationship.

Male patients should continue to be shaved regularly, by the nurse if no other family member is able or willing to do it. An electric, or even better, battery-operated shaver can be a useful addition in the nursing bag, enabling the patient to be shaved with a minimum of fuss. He should be given a wet shave if that is his preference.

The maintenance of the usual hair-style is most important for the patient's morale, especially for ladies. Efforts should be made to keep the hair in good condition—perhaps the patient can be taken out to the hairdresser, or the hairdresser may visit if the special circumstances are explained. If the hair can be washed just prior to the patient's final decline, it will help to maintain his appearance during those last days. This is important for the relatives, too, as they watch the patient die.

Mouth Care

Normal care of the mouth by tooth brushing (unless the patient has dentures) should continue for as long as possible. Monilial infection occurs frequently. The mouth should be inspected with a torch at every visit, and treatment should be quickly organized if the white spots of thrush are seen.

Foot Care

For an ill and weak patient washing the feet can be most soothing and refreshing. It is not just Biblical characters who benefit from having their feet soaked in a bowl of warm, comforting water. Many people are ashamed of no longer being able to cut their own toenails. An enthusiastic nurse with a pair of good nail clippers can make a patient feel thoroughly pampered. It is rare to find toenails which, following a good soaking, cannot be adequately dealt with by a nurse. Dying patients cannot wait for a chiropodist who may not be available for weeks or months.

Pressure Areas

If the patient is only comfortable in an upright position, perhaps because of dyspnoea or overweight, he is more likely to develop pressure sores. However, the majority of patients will remain relatively mobile and entirely free from sores. If, late in the illness, the skin does break, it should be no more than minimal. There are techniques for calculating the likely occurrence of pressure sores (Norton 1975) and numerous methods of prevention and treatment. PREVENTION is the aim.

Air-rings do help some patients. Sheepskins may also help, but only if they are maintained in good condition. A bed cradle to support the mountain of blankets which cover some beds may prevent heels from becoming sore. In addition a pillow can be placed under the patient's calves, just allowing the heels to hang clear of the mattress.

Encouraging a somewhat 'bullying' attitude in the care giver towards the patient can be a great help in prevention. This takes the form of strict attention to regular turning at 4-hourly intervals, or 2-hourly if necessary and possible. Once a spouse has seen and learned how comfortable the patient can be on his side, she will be enthusiastic in the execution of such a programme. When the skin is particularly at risk, the patient should be turned by the nurse at the end of each visit, to ensure he is off his sacrum properly, for at least a few minutes — if only until the nurse is out of the house. A certain amount of hectoring the patient about changing his position is justified because it can prevent so many future problems. Following an explanation, these problems will usually be appreciated by the patient.

A *large-cell* ripple mattress appears to offer substantial protection of pressure areas for an emaciated and immobile patient. Some people are reluctant at first to use it — often through fear of electrocution or of running up a large electricity bill. The mattress may be uncomfortable if it is not correctly adjusted. It is vital to remember to adjust the dial on the motor to 'large cell'. If inadvertently set for 'standard or small' it will not work properly. The large-cell mattress has a tendency to puncture relatively frequently and should be checked at every visit; the family also can be shown how to check it by placing the hand over two or three cells for several minutes to determine that the correct rhythm of inflation and deflation is taking place. The family should be reminded not to catch the tubing in the bedclothes and to position the lead so that it cannot be tripped over. If the patient feels that the mattress is too hard it should be adjusted to a lighter setting.

The main disadvantage of the large cell mattress is that it is 36 inches wide. This may leave a spouse only 18 inches of bed on which to sleep. Some families will manage, others will produce a spare bed. Where neither is possible and the couple are obviously reluctant to have their sleeping habits rearranged, the nurse may have abandon the idea of using the ripple mattress. A Spenco siliconized mattress may be a suitable alternative. It is washable, easily portable and has no leads or wires; one side has a waterproof covering, the other cotton/polyester. Further information can be obtained from: Spenco Medical Ltd, Tanyard Lane, Steyning, West Sussex, BN4 3RJ.

A painful, superficial pressure sore may be helped by the application of xylocaine antiseptic urethral gel. The resulting local anaesthesia, which will make the patient more comfortable, may aggravate the condition, however, as he will be less likely to make the effort to change his position.

There is considerable controversy concerning the best treatment for deep pressure sores. The use of energy to prevent pressure sores is much less than the output necessary to treat them—one of the principle reasons for my abiding interest in the former.

Fungating Lesions

Here, too, opinions on the best form of treatment will vary. The following are by no means a complete catalogue of the possibilities; the intention is to suggest several methods which the reader may wish to incorporate into her practice where appropriate.

It is important that a swab is taken for microbiology culture, even if this entails considerable effort to organize. If the lesion can be helped by the appropriate systemic antibiotic, time will ultimately be saved with the improvement of the condition. A course of metronidazole (Flagyl) may be used empirically as it can be remarkably effective in reducing the smell. A smelly, ulcerating breast may also be helped by twice daily dressings using plain, live yoghurt. The acid environment produced and lactobacilli combine to combat an offensive odour. The usual wound cleansing should be performed prior to the application of yoghurt.

If moist dressings regularly leak through to the clothing, the area should be covered by a piece of polythene (domestic cling-film or a piece cut from a polythene bag are ideal). It is sealed round three sides, leaving some space at the top for air exchange. This procedure is much appreciated by whoever does the household washing.

Denidor dressing pads contain a charcoal preparation and are used in conjunction with the gauze dressing. They help to absorb an unpleasant smell. A few drops of Nilodor on the bed linen or dressing (but not on the skin), may also help the elimination of odour. If half-strength Eusol is used for wound cleansing, any lotion remaining after the date of expiry, which *should have been marked* on the bottle when it was made up, should be discarded.

Adrenaline 1:1000 may be added to a gauze dressing and applied to stop slow venous oozing of a fungating breast ulcer (see Oxycel, Chapter 3).

Diet

The patient should be encouraged to eat as he likes. However, if 'what he likes' consists solely of tea and biscuits, other suggestions should be offered, such as fresh fruit juice, egg in milk with brandy, egg custard or other light, nourishing snacks. In London's East End, a pint of jellied eels may dramatically raise a patient's morale. Sometimes an anorexic patient is keeping rigidly to a diet imposed upon him years earlier by the medical staff—perhaps a low salt or low carbohydrate diet. Following consultation with a doctor, the nurse can usually release the patient from this restriction and thus permit greater freedom of choice of food.

Anorexia may be increased by an anxious spouse who, having fed her husband for forty years, feels that she can 'feed him out' of this illness and offers large quantities of food, far in excess of his appetite. She must be urged to provide him with small portions only, to tempt the appetite. A female patient may be reluctant to eat unappetizing food lovingly prepared by an inexpert husband. The nurse has to approach these problems very tactfully without upsetting the household caterer.

Some patients like to take Complan when they are unable to tolerate ordinary food. This may satisfy patient and spouse when they learn that two or three drinks of it daily provide a good proportion of total nutritional requirements. Although it may appear expensive, it should be remembered that less money is being spent on other foods such as meat and fish which proportionately are much dearer. Food which has been liquidized in a blender, or a proprietary baby food, may be acceptable for some patients—particularly those with oesophageal problems.

Many people believe that alcohol and medication are incompatible. For dying patients this is not so—they may be encouraged to take a moderate amount of alcohol if they wish. Sherry before meals is helpful as an appetite stimulant. A favourite tipple of whisky or brandy often promotes a good night's sleep. Patients are unlikely to over-indulge with alcohol and frequently report that they no longer enjoy their regular pint or two of beer as they used to.

Bowel Management

Patients may initially express surprise and embarrassment on being closely questioned about their bowel habits, but within a short time will volunteer the information almost as you walk in the door. Accepting a 'yes' or 'no' answer to the question 'have your bowels worked?' is inadequate. At each visit information is needed about the frequency, consistency and amount of the bowel action(s). Some patients will only learn the value of this questioning after they have suffered the consequences of taking bowel medication unreliably or withholding information about the true state of affairs.

Giving an enema should almost never be necessary. If it is, the most effective is the disposable variety which has a long tube incorporated. A rectal catheter should be attached to the nozzle to ensure that the fluid reaches to the splenic flexure of the colon —not just two inches into the rectum.

Dulcolax (bisacodyl) suppositories and generous amounts of laxatives are much less traumatic than an enema for a sick patient, and are usually effective within a few days.

However, if the patient presents with a faecal impaction, manual removal will usually be necessary. Generally, the patient will be able to use the toilet or commode, a position which naturally utilizes the earth's gravitational force. This is much more effective than the traditional left lateral position. It is essential to be totally aware throughout of maintaining the dignity of the patient. This is largely achieved by acknowledging that it is not a very nice procedure for him, that you are sorry for his sake, that he need not worry about your feelings, but that he will very quickly feel much better. Most patients with an impaction feel so terrible, that they have, sadly, often reached a point of not caring what is done as long as their misery is relieved.

The patient is asked to sit (not bend) forward on the toilet or commode. The nurse stands at his left side and inserts her lubricated, gloved index finger into the rectum, from behind. Extra support may be given to the patient, who may be quite weak, by the nurse's left hand being placed against his left shoulder. In a sitting position the patient is more likely to have a peristaltic action and be able to help in the expulsion of the faeces. The pulling action of the nurse should coincide with and facilitate the pushing action of the patient. The conclusion of a successful procedure produces nearly as much relief for the nurse and family as it does for the patient!

Occasionally, manual evacuation will have to be performed under a general anaesthetic, in which case the doctor may administer intravenous diazepam (Valium).

Urinary Tract

Patients are sometimes troubled by oliguria, which may be a symptom of impending renal failure or simply be caused by dehydration, for example, during hot weather. Oliguria may also result from ascites and/or oedema. Renal failure can be confirmed by a negative result from a residual catheterization.

Incontinence in male patients may be relieved with condom drainage, but success depends partly upon the effective application of the condom and partly on the cooperation of the patient. If he is confused he is likely to pull it off.

Urinary retention, if not relieved by the usual simple methods, should be treated by catheterization. Where possible, this need should be anticipated, so that the equipment is available and prior permission obtained from the doctor to carry out the procedure. If the patient is male, and the problem urgent, a female nurse should have no qualms about catheterizing the patient, provided he has no disease of the bladder or prostate. It is unnecessary to prolong his suffering while waiting for a male nurse to be brought in.

Maximum effectiveness, minimum fuss is a useful thought when performing most nursing procedures for dying patients. While attention to hygiene and prevention of infection are important, the comfort of the patient should not be sacrificed to a long, meticulous catheterization technique. He will usually not live long enough to be affected by urinary infections. In most cities in Britain, tap water, which contains relatively few bacteria, is adequate for inflating the balloon of the catheter. It is unnecessary to send relatives into a panic by asking for cooled, boiled water, which they will try to produce within minutes. The nurse may, however, have sterile ampoules of water — care is needed that they are not inadvertently crushed either in transit or storage.

When a patient's probable life expectancy is only a few weeks, it is unnecessary to keep changing the catheter, unless it presents problems of blockage or leakage. Infection is more likely to be introduced with regular recatheterization, as complete sterilization of the urethral orifice is not possible. Xylocaine antiseptic urethral gel may be used for female as well as male patients, in order to minimize the introduction of infection and to reduce the discomfort which often persists for the first hour or two following catheterization. The gel should be squeezed onto the catheter just prior to insertion (into a female patient).

If the patient has a urinary tract infection and experiences difficulty in swallowing or retaining oral antibiotics, bladder irrigation with noxytiolin (Noxyflex) is usually effective. It is, however, very expensive, and should therefore be stored and used according to the directions.

Relatives should be shown how to empty the drainage bag, which to them may seem quite alarming. They will also require reassurance that there is nothing to worry about if air appears to be going up the drainage tube. Another fear of relatives is that the catheter will fall out—describing the balloon will usually allay those fears. Finally, they should be instructed to take care not to squash or kink the tubing or place the bag higher than the patient. These details are so routine to nurses that it is easy to forget how frightening such things appear to the public— especially if a loved one is at the other end of the contraption.

Catheterization should never be forced on a patient who does not want it. Often, though, it is the family who resist because they do not want the patient 'interfered' with. They will usually agree once they begin to see the effect of incontinence on the patient's skin, and feel the wearing effect on themselves of extra changing and laundering of bed linen.

Before catheterization is required, a bedpan, urinal or commode should be provided as appropriate. Someone who is dying cannot wait for a week or two for equipment to be delivered—he will need it immediately or by the following day. Where the bureaucratic system moves slowly, it must be somehow educated to appreciate that the needs of the dying patient are immediate—by the day after tomorrow the patient may be dead. The district nurse should not need to use her valuable time to collect and deliver the equipment herself— time which would be better spent with the patient and his family.

Recreation, Mobilization and Sleep

Another hospice motto 'live until you die' can be very meaningful if a patient is lying lethargically in bed, waiting for death to seize him and drag him off to the dreaded unknown. Mobilization may need to be encouraged (or gently discouraged, if excessive), and may be achieved to the point where the patient is able to get dressed and go out. It may be helpful to set specific goals such as a favourite outing to the seaside or a visit to the local pub. It may be necessary to allow the patient to realize slowly that he is still able to wash his face, still able to sit on the edge of the bed, still able to walk to the bathroom, and so on, until maximum improvement is achieved. The process may, of course, be assisted by using medication to control symptoms. However, if the patient is very ill and weak he should not be forced to sit in a chair because it is considered 'to be good for him'.

Boredom and lethargy may result from the patient being unable to practise a favourite hobby, usually because of weakness. He may never have developed any hobbies. A lady may believe that because she is now unable to cook, scrub and sew she is useless, a burden and would be better off dead. A gentleman's similar feelings may be centred round his inability to paint the house, crawl under the car, dig the garden or get to the pub. Helping a patient to feel like a useful, contributing member of society is most important.

The nurse, with the occupational or recreational therapist, can devise activities appropriate to the patient's strengths and abilities. However, many people will resent and resist recreational therapy for its own sake. If a charitable outlet can be found for the completed efforts then enthusiasm is much more likely to be aroused. Frequently, a simple task such as knitting squares to be made into blankets is pursued with relish by patients too weak mentally or physically to do anything more energetic. The squares may come in a variety of shapes and sizes, but it is good to see a new zeal arise in a previously morose patient. Many male patients are also able to join the knitting brigade (although some will proudly present a beautiful pile of squares knitted by their wives instead!). However, such wives are usually happy to perform this extra task, relieved that something has aroused their husband's interest. Patients often experience loss of concentration or interest in reading and the more passive exercise of listening to music or cassettes of 'talking books', may be more acceptable.

The combination of recreational activity and general mobilization will usually improve the patient's sleeping habits.

Fear of insomnia will often produce insomnia. It can help if the patient is confidently reassured that his body will ensure it gets the amount of sleep it needs, and that it is likely his sleep requirements have diminished. He may still be dissatisfied because he has nothing with which to occupy himself on waking at 5 am after six hours' sleep, while the rest of the house slumbers on. Going to bed later, not sleeping too much in the day or a book to dip into when awake, may improve the situation. Night sedation may need to be prescribed, changed or adjusted.

Other Considerations

Routine 'TPR and BP' observations are *never* necessary for patients who are dying. Observation of the change of respiratory rate is necessary as death approaches in order to explain to the family as fully as possible about the patient's condition. When the patient is pyrexial this should be obvious from the sense of touch—a thermometer should not be necessary. It is usually sufficient to know that the patient is pyrexial, not the exact point reached on the thermometer.

There is no place either for blood pressure recordings, unless the patient has considerable time to live and requires appropriate treatment. Knowing that a patient's blood pressure is 70/? is no help to anyone when he is breathing his last. It is just an uncomfortable procedure for the patient (and this must be pointed out to relatives if they believe the nurse should still be checking it). On the other hand, taking the pulse causes no discomfort and can supply useful information as to the likelihood of imminent death, by changes in rate and volume.

A patient with whom I discussed this book urged me to mention nurses' visiting arrangements. Initially, the nurse may need to visit daily until the various problems are dealt with and a relationship is established with the patient and family. Then there may be a plateau of, perhaps, several weeks when contact is required no more than three times a week, and often less. As the patient's condition deteriorates the frequency of visits naturally increases up to perhaps three times a day. A community nurse's caseload contains a high proportion of chronically sick patients, whose condition varies little from month to month. It is necessary to guard against adopting the same assumption about a dying patient. It is important to recognize when a patient with carcinomatosis is at a plateau phase, because this can change fairly quickly. It is unwise to settle into a routine of fortnightly or monthly contacts because a patient may have developed a chest infection and died in the interim.

The patient and family must know when to expect the next contact from the nurse (Goodwin 1982). It is cruel to end a visit by saying 'Goodbye, I'll be in touch next week sometime'. There is an appropriate time for the next contact and that *must* be established before the end of the visit (or telephone conversation). Patients and families understand that it is difficult for a busy nurse to state a particular time, but it is inexcusable not to specify a day, and enormously increases the anxiety in the household.

Some of the comments in this chapter may appear elementary. However, from time to time it is useful to reflect on basic approaches to patients, in order to perceive the need to modify our practices.

Chapter 5

Care in the Last Few Days

> If you would indeed behold the spirit of death,
> open your heart wide unto the body of life.
> For life and death are one,
> even as the river and the sea are one.
>
> *The Prophet* K Gibran

The final phase of life for many is heralded by the onset of a chest infection and a change in the level of consciousness. Nurses will have seen this sequence of events on many occasions, but for the patient and his family it may be the *first* time. If we do not remain aware of that, we cannot properly care for the patient or his family. We have all experienced the sense of privilege when nursing a dying patient: that privilege is abused if we do not treat each situation as unique.

This planet contains around 4,000 million people — each have two eyes, a nose and a mouth. Incredibly, each face is different and each birth is different. Similarly, each death will be different, and almost totally unpredictable. The more I work with dying patients and observe the infinite variety of characteristics each presents, the less certain have I become about predicting the sequence of events prior to death.

One patient may appear to be well, with a considerable time to live, but then die rapidly within days. Another may give the impression of being about to die, but instead improves daily and subsequently lives for several more months — discarding much of his medication as he rallies. A patient with Cheyne-Stokes respiration may look moribund, but nevertheless live for another week. It can be difficult to decide whether or not to remain in the home of a patient who looks as if he is about to die. It could mean a 24 or 48-hour wait, or the patient may die five minutes after the nurse has left the house.

In fact the aim should be to see that the patient is peaceful and comfortable and that the family is prepared and able to cope with the death whenever it occurs, although it is usually a relief for the family if the nurse is present at the death. Sometimes in fact I have a strong urge to rearrange the order of visits and because of this may arrive at a home, much to the relief of the family, just as the patient is dying. This sixth sense is experienced by most people but often ignored. If we obeyed it more often, it is likely that we would more frequently find ourselves in the right place at the right time.

The direction of care, particularly in the last few days, should be towards 'crisis prevention' rather than 'crisis intervention'. The degree to which this is accomplished can make the difference between the family managing or the patient having to be admitted precipitately to hospital. Crisis prevention is why the timing and frequency of visits is critical. A family cannot be expected to cope if they have to suffer the anxiety of a succession of new problems such as vomiting, incontinence or confusion, because 'the nurse is visiting the day after tomorrow and she will sort it out then'. Families do not like to be a nuisance, continually on the phone to the doctor or nurse. Of course, it is not possible to anticipate every change in condition. It is reasonable for the family to have to phone on occasion but it should *not* be the norm. *Reliable* arrangements should be established so that relatives can contact either the doctor or the nurse without delay by day or night.

Nursing Care

As the patient's condition changes and deteriorates, care must be tailored to his needs. It is also important to remember that even an apparently unconscious patient can sometimes hear what is being said and should be told of nursing procedures before they are performed.

It is difficult to nurse an unconscious patient adequately on a narrow settee. Just before that state is reached, he should, if possible, be transferred to a proper bed. If there is room in the home, it may be useful to borrow a bed from the local authority. Frequently, however, these beds are high and old, probably discarded years ago by the local hospital, now upgraded with adjustable beds.

It may have become necessary for the nurse to wash the patient or help the spouse to do so. If he is very weak it may tire him less to wash areas such as the back or legs on different days. Likewise, it may be better to change his clothing or bed linen at different times, unless profuse sweating or incontinence precludes it. Limbs should be well supported when being washed, to avoid increasing his fatigue.

The patient will probably need to be made comfortable on his side, and the family can be taught how to do this without hurting the patient or themselves.

Basic nursing training has instilled in us the necessity of sitting a patient upright in bed in order to prevent a chest infection. When a very ill patient is dying peacefully of pneumonia, no prevention is possible. Nothing looks (and probably feels) more distressing than a semi-conscious patient lolling around in an upright position, even if it gratifies the aesthetic tastes and training of the nurse. A rattling chest will often be relieved without medication simply by turning the patient on to his side. Some unconscious patients, particularly those who have carcinoma of the bronchus, are restless and distressed when turned on to a particular side. This may be because the remaining lung, which is now infected, is trying to cope with oxygenation of the body and is being compressed by the diseased lung. The patient should still be moved, but not onto the side which causes discomfort.

The pillows should be arranged in an inverted V-shape, so that at least two are tucked between his head and shoulder to prevent his shoulder being squashed. The lower arm should not be restricted by his body but be gently pulled clear of it. Hips are lifted towards the edge of the bed, and the upper leg crossed over the lower. Both legs should be bent; a pillow between them will provide better support and keep the skin surfaces from rubbing. The back should also be supported with pillows. With the patient in this position, the relatives will usually give a little sigh and say 'Oh, he does look so comfortable, now!'. In fact, this is often one way of measuring the efficacy of the nursing care given.

Because it is often difficult to know when a patient will die, such nursing care should continue until the end, unless there are exceptional circumstances. A 20-stone patient on a 2′ 6″ "Put-U-Up" bed is likely to prove an exceptional circumstance.

Sometimes a relative will say 'It's a shame to disturb him!'. It is in fact a shame not to do so. Probably he is sleeping much of the time and getting adequate rest, which should be explained to the family. Pressure areas can become black and bleeding within 24 hours if the patient is not moved, and only rarely can this be justified. It is quite possible that the patient may live for several more days. If the family are helping with the nursing care the memory of those blackened and bleeding areas will probably remain with them forever. A slow, gentle approach to the patient will cause him little disturbance and help to maintain, to some degree, the body which he still inhabits. It is easy not to realize how almost unrecognizable the patient has become to the family in perhaps only a few months. Allowing them to witness the body literally bleeding and falling apart is cruel. When time seems short and the list of patients still to be visited is long, it can be particularly tempting to agree to leave the patient 'until tomorrow' or some other time. That may be condemning the patient to lie in a pool of urine or faeces for 24 hours or colleagues to be called out later in the day by a distressed family who have discovered the incontinence themselves.

A male patient should continue to be shaved—just enough to make him presentable to the family—unless they would prefer that he were not shaved.

If the patient is pyrexial and sweating it may be necessary to remove most of the blankets, in which he may have been swathed by a well-meaning family to prevent him 'catching cold'. The reason for removing the blankets should therefore be explained to the family. Fans and tepid-sponging are often helpful. A draw-sheet may also help to keep the patient fresh, and will save on the household washing and make the nursing easier to carry out. Relatives may have to be discouraged from enthusiastically cutting up their best linen for this purpose. With a bit of persuasion most wives can produce an old, worn sheet which she may have been reluctant for the nurse to see.

Dentures should be removed before the patient becomes

unconscious. Foam-stick applicators (Smith and Nephew) dipped in a frequently-changed glass of water, will usually keep the mouth clean. A solution of bicarbonate of soda may be used if preferred or if the mouth is very dirty. Vaseline applied to the lips will help prevent them cracking. Once the mouth is clean the family can be shown how to continue the care—it is a relatively simple procedure which they can perform for their loved one, particularly if they are unable to help with the rest of the physical care. The foamstick applicators are available in supplementary packs of 5 (1,000 per box). Their use will obviate the need to discard the whole of the plastic mouth tray pack each time the foamsticks it contains are used up. This could prove a considerable financial saving.

Diet

Gradually the patient will stop taking solid food and be able to tolerate fluids only. Milky drinks should be followed by a few sips of water in order to keep the mouth as fresh as possible. When the patient is unable to take fluids from a cup or spoon, the foamstick applicators are again very useful as he may be able to suck fluid off them.

Bowel Care

Some degree of anticipation of approaching death is important. Nursing management is much more difficult and distressing for the family if the patient is leaking faeces in his last days. To prevent this, regular bowel movements (every 3–4 days) should be maintained, with suppositories if necessary. The aim is for the patient to have a final bowel movement just prior to the point when he is unable to get out of bed onto the commode.

Management of Urinary Output

Anticipation is needed here also, to prevent the possibility of a ruined mattress and further expense for the family. A draw-mackintosh should be in situ under the draw-sheet *before* the patient is incontinent of urine. It can usually be discreetly slipped under when the patient is too weak to notice and be affronted by it, but while he is still continent. An ideal draw-mac is usually readily available in every home in the form of a large domestic black polythene bag which can be cut down one side and opened out across the bottom.

It may be appropriate to consider catheterization of the patient around this time—or just after he has become incontinent. Even if the patient is catheterized, plastic sheeting will still be required in case the catheter should leak. If the patient is male and very peaceful, a urinal in situ may preclude catheterization. The urinal should be wrapped in some form of wadding to prevent chafing of the skin around the genitalia.

Medication

The patient's medication will tail off naturally as he becomes unable to swallow it—probably dispensing with the larger tablets first. Unconscious patients are often able to appreciate pain and likely to have withdrawal symptoms if an opiate is stopped suddenly. Essential medication such as pain or anticonvulsant treatment should therefore be continued until the patient's death. Again, the foamstick applicators can be excellent—the patient being able to suck medicine from them. An alternative mode of administration is necessary if the patient cannot swallow; this should be decided upon and organized *before the need arises* to prevent unnecessary delay and extra suffering for everyone. The majority of patients are likely to be able to continue with oral mixtures to within 4 hours of death and therefore not require alternative medication.

The use of suppositories should always be considered before resorting to injections (Gusterson *et al.* 1979), which can be distressing for everyone if the patient is very emaciated. Absorption of injections is affected by lymphoedema and effective plasma levels are more difficult to achieve (Vere 1978). Suppositories cannot be administered effectively if the rectum is full of faeces, hence the desirability of a bowel action just prior to the patient reaching this point. One member of the family will usually be prepared to give the suppositories. Precise instruction is necessary—it is useless to provide gloves, suppositories and lubricant and expect her to cope. It must be explained why the left lateral position is used whenever possible. If the suppositories are wrapped the giver should be reminded to remove the wrapper — it is not unknown for an error to occur in this respect. It is also a great help to say that, as the suppository is pushed in some resistance will be felt from the ring of muscle (anal sphincter), after which it will slip in easily and should be inserted as far as the index finger will reach. Another important point is to mention the possibility of the suppository popping out before it is fully inserted, and that it should simply be popped in again. Being present while the first suppositories are given will ensure a successful and happy conclusion to the teaching session.

Medication currently available in suppository form includes:

> prochlorperazine (Stemetil) 25 mg
> chlorpromazine (Largarctil) 100 mg — equivalent to about 25 mg orally
> cyclizine (Valoid, Marzine) 50 mg
> diazepam (Valium) 5 and 10 mg
> oxycodone pectinate 30 mg
> morphine 5–200 mg.

The possible onset of confusion and restlessness must be explained to the family, who should be told to phone for help if it occurs — not just sit and wait until they are visited.

Restlessness or confusion in the terminal stages usually results from a combination of factors, including pneumonia, hypoxia and electrolyte imbalance; a full bowel or bladder, an uncomfortable position or pain should also always be considered. Whatever the cause, the situation must be alleviated if the family are to have sufficient confidence in themselves and the professional care givers to keep the patient at home in these last few days.

Some patients will require larger doses of sedative than normal because there is often a degree of malabsorption at this stage as a result of circulatory failure (Lamerton 1979). If injectable sedatives are to be used, methotrimiprazine (Nozinan, previously Veractil) 25–50 mg can first be tried; it can be mixed in the same syringe with medication such as methadone or atropine and 25 mg is contained in half the volume of, and is approximately twice as effective as, 25 mg of chlorpromazine (Largactil). If the patient remains restless he may be given 200 mg phenobarbitone (1 ml), which is usually much more effective than diazepam (Valium) 10 mg and half the volume. The dose of phenobarbitone may be doubled, if necessary, or a combination of drugs used. Both diazepam and phenobarbitone have to be given separately from other medication.

It is likely that, initially, the level of sedation will need to be changed frequently—perhaps several times a day—until the patient is peaceful. It is therefore essential that the doctor should have prescribed beforehand a range of drugs and doses so that as the nurse monitors the patient's condition she can vary the amount of sedation. If the nurse is not organized to be able to do this, a distressing situation will be prolonged and the patient will be better served by having the doctor visit instead of her.

If intramuscular analgesia is required at this stage, methadone has the advantage of longer duration of action than either morphine or diamorphine, so that an 8-hourly injection regime can usually be organized, incorporating sedation and atropine or hyoscine (to dry up the 'rattle') as necessary. The latter should ideally only be given when the patient is unconscious so that he does not have to suffer the discomfort of an intensely dry mouth.

In some areas of the country, syringe drivers are available; these are small, portable, battery-operated infusion pumps which enable a measured amount of medication to be given subcutaneously via a syringe over a 24-hour period. As the insertion site of the needle may remain patent for several days, the use of a syringe driver means that the patient does not have to be punctured frequently by needles, the family (or the nurse) is freed from the necessity of giving suppositories, and the nursing team has more scope within the 24 hours to organize the timing and frequency of visits. Very occasionally the pump will stop and, therefore, the family must be shown how to check its operation. The problem may be a flat battery or a blocked needle, but in practice the pump rarely goes wrong. At the time of writing the cost of one of these pumps is approximately £300—further information may be obtained from Graseby

Dynamics Ltd., Park Avenue, Bushey, Watford, Herts WD2 2BW, England.

Night Sitters

A night sitter, particularly for the last few nights, will often mean the difference between the patient dying peacefully at home with a satisfied family, or being bundled into hospital and perhaps dying within 24 hours, leaving a guilt-ridden family.

Currently there are three principal ways of providing a night sitter. In some areas the Marie Curie Memorial Foundation supplies a nurse free of charge. In others, the Foundation will share with the health district the cost of employing an agency nurse; she may be a marvellous support to the family, or otherwise—it is not unknown for an agency nurse to sleep in an armchair while the family tosses and turns, wondering if everything is all right! The least effective way, unfortunately, is to have a sitter supplied by a health district offering a 24-hour nursing service. There is often uncertainty right into the evening about whether or not a nurse will be available on that particular night, or there may be two patients requiring a night sitter and only one is available. Staff shortages, sickness and annual leave are the main deciding factors. Frequently, the sitter will arrive at the house at midnight after completing her evening rounds, and leave again at 5 am for her morning visits. Thus by the time the family have settled themselves and shown the nurse how to help herself to a cup of tea, etc, it is almost time for them to get up again, as the nurse may want to help in washing and turning the patient before she leaves. In these circumstances the family may be better off with the certain knowledge of an evening visit than the uncertainty of a night sitter.

Spiritual Needs

Most practising Roman Catholic families will have been in regular contact with their priest. Some patients who have not practised their religion, will want to 'unlapse' before they die, and renew contact with the church. Asking a patient or family if a priest should be contacted must be done with great tact; some welcome the suggestion, others may greatly resent it.

Because many different religions are currently practised in Great Britain, district nurses may be unsure of how to meet particular religious needs. In order to give the appropriate help and advice at the time of death, the nurse should have previously spoken to the family or to the minister of the particular religion. The degree of orthodox observance will often vary with each family, and the nurse must be prepared for this so that she can act appropriately whatever the circumstances.

The nurse's role in the spiritual care of the patient will depend on her own beliefs and those of the patient. She must never try to discuss religion with a patient who does not wish to do so. Where a spiritual rapport does exist, the nurse/patient relationship may be enhanced by discussion or praying together. If the nurse feels comfortable, the family is often appreciative of some simple prayers being said when the patient is unconscious. The Lord's Prayer and the 23rd psalm are usually appropriate (Lamerton 1977).

After the Death

Following the family's initial distress at the patient's death, the nurse's calm and confident approach should help to support the family, who are likely to be very confused: each situation will be different. There may be an old aunt who has seen it all before and organizes everyone and everything. Often there is a relative — perhaps a son — who wishes to do his duty, but is not sure what that is. Occasionally, there is an elderly spouse with few relatives or friends who sits stunned and alone in a corner. A cup of tea in the true British tradition usually helps — whatever the situation.

The family are often relieved if the nurse offers to contact the undertaker and general practitioner for them. She may need to suggest an undertaker if the family has no ideas or preferences. She can then telephone the undertaker to notify him, in advance of the death certificate being issued by the doctor. Subsequently, all the family have to do is to ring back later, after the doctor has visited, and say that 'Mr Smith is ready to be taken away now'.

The nurse should have previously ensured that a doctor had seen the patient in the previous two weeks, otherwise there will be legal complications about issuing the certificate. Involvement of the coroner and a possible post-mortem could result, with great distress to the family. The doctor should be encouraged to visit the family (with the certificate) rather than vice versa as they will have many errands to run in the following days. It is important to reassure the family that although they will have a lot to do they will be given enough information at each step of the way in order to know what to do next. Being able to tell them where to register the death and the registrar's hours of business is usually one of the first steps.

Last Offices

Last offices should be performed with a minimum of fuss to prevent needless further distress to the family. Some families, however, will present the nurse with a set of new clothing and the body must be washed and dressed according to their wishes, but usually it is necessary only to straighten and tidy the body. (The nurse should always refer to the body as 'Mr Smith' or 'your husband' etc, when speaking to the relatives.) The undertaker will always prepare the body, however many orifices have been carefully packed with cotton wool by the nurse. Obviously, if the patient has vomited or been incontinent he must be washed.

Blankets should be removed from the bed, leaving just the top sheet and counterpane. Any radiators or heaters are switched off and a window opened. The head should be supported on one or two pillows and the hair arranged as naturally as possible. If the eyes are not closed sufficiently, this should be done using a technique that is likely to be the least alarming to the family. A small amount of Micropore tape (about 1 mm wide) on the outer edge of each eye just sufficient to hold the lids together, is a method I have found useful. The aim is to maintain a normal facial appearance as much as possible. Dentures are inserted and the jaw supported. A simple and effective way is to find an object such as a dry bar of soap, a small bottle or a cigarette packet, which can then be used as a wedge between the chin and top of the sternum. The sheet is then pulled up sufficiently just to cover the chin, leaving the patient's face normal, without being distorted by scarves or bandages. Dressings should be renewed as necessary, catheters and jewellery removed.

By this time the body should have the appearance of peace and repose and the family can be encouraged (not forced) to say 'goodbye' while the nurse is in attendance. They are greatly comforted by seeing the loved one look so peaceful. At some point, when the spouse is seated, she should be handed the wedding ring. This is often an intensely emotional moment which may bring forth the tears, which have perhaps been held back up to that point. Occasionally, the relatives may prefer rings or other jewellery to be left on the body.

It is usually better not to begin to remove equipment from the house, but to return on another occasion. Before leaving, the nurse might ask to be informed of the funeral arrangements, when they have been made. Families appreciate it very much when the nurse can attend the funeral, or at least visit the house for ten minutes or so just before the cortège leaves for the cemetery. Alternatively, if a church service is being held locally, the nurse may be able to attend that. Where there may be only one or two mourners she should consider it her duty to attend the funeral, which in any case is a natural and fitting conclusion to the care of her patient.

Chapter 6

Meeting the Patient's Non-Physical Needs

> Accept the life that's given to you,
> That's half the battle won,
> With it will bring peace of mind,
> You'll always see the sun.
>
> You'll always see a smiling face,
> A hand reach out for you.
> Take it and be grateful
> For it will help you through.
>
>   ER (A patient)

I met Mrs R., the patient who wrote this poem, only three times before she was admitted to hospital and I was unfortunately unable to keep in contact with her. Those three meetings intensely reflected several characteristics I have observed to a greater or lesser degree in many patients. The first visit revealed an upset and anxious person who was very pleased to see a nurse. By the next day she had transformed into the calm, accepting person who wrote the poems heading some of these chapters. She talked freely of death and acceptance and radiated enough joy to raise my spirits considerably. Shyly she produced a large sheaf of about 40 poems. She said that she had been inspired to write them in the course of one year — never having written before or since that time. I felt humble and honoured to have them given to me. The modest East End of London background from which she came does not produce many poets.

The next time I visited Mrs R., a few days later, it was hard to believe she was the same person. The anxious side of her personality was again ruling supreme. She couldn't manage at home, the family couldn't cope. She claimed that if she went back to hospital everything would be made better. The whole family was resolute. The only contribution I could make to this dramatically changed situation was to facilitate the admission arrangements, which the family had already initiated.

When I began in this work I optimistically assumed that my patients would spend their final days in a perpetual state of blissful acceptance. By the end of my first year I considered myself to be dreadfully inept as my expectations were far from being fulfilled. Gradually I learned that total acceptance of death and dying is not experienced by all people, and that in common with the rest of the population, dying people are prone to mood changes. To 'get out of bed on the wrong side' is a readily acceptable phenomenon. We should not be surprised if our patients do likewise—usually with far greater reason.

People have talked of the necessity of coming to terms with one's own death, before being able to help others do the same. I believe it is only possible to prepare for one's own death, when faced with that reality. Each of us tackles the prospect in a unique way—imagining it, or prefabricating any other situation, can never be compared with reality. Lack of experience does not mean that we cannot help others—it is not necessary to have had a baby in order to become a midwife, although experience does, of course, enhance understanding.

There are many ways of helping a patient, but what is important is that alongside our professional image, we should also present the face of humanity and friendship. It is likely that most patients will have received, and been grateful for, the professional care given during the course of the illness; but often the friendship has been insufficient or absent. Gibran's wonderful poetry can illuminate the meaning of the word, and indicate how we can improve the care we offer:

> '. . . Your friend is your needs answered' . . .
> '. . . And when he is silent your heart ceases
>   not to listen to his heart;' . . .
> '. . . And let your best be for your friend.' . . .
> *The Prophet*

How well we would answer the needs of our patient if we

listened to him even when he is silent and gave only of our best, whatever the circumstances. When a person is dying we should work especially at all these three aspects of caring, even if success appears limited.

Frequently a nurse will give of her best but feel she has failed because the patient has remained anxious or depressed. In fact, the patient will usually feel considerably relieved and be grateful for the visit, having off-loaded his problem onto the nurse. Following such a meeting some action may or may not be appropriate: this dilemma is aptly portrayed by the following rhyme:

> 'For every ill beneath the sun
> There is some remedy, or none.
> Should there be one, resolve to find it;
> If not, submit, and never mind it.'
> *Anon.*

To continue to brood over something which cannot be changed will affect the nurse's approach to other patients. If a nurse does have particular difficulty with a patient, it is often helpful for other team members to relieve her of some of the visits. This will also facilitate the sharing of views and information which is of itself most valuable.

There is much talk of professional 'burn-out', particularly in the USA (Maslack 1976). It seems to stem from the sentimental idea that one should be weighed down by the burden of a patient's life and problems. This is, of course, unnecessary and unrealistic. We become emotional and weepy watching a sad scene on the cinema screen. We are doing our patients a disservice by allowing ourselves to react in a similar manner to a sad scene on the stage of life by exhibiting an identical response. If we reacted with tears to all the misery and injustice in the world, a new Noah's flood would cover the face of the earth. However, this does not mean that a nurse should never cry with a family; relatives may be much comforted by it provided that the nurse does not become incapacitated by her own outpouring. Actually, in Britain, we appear to be able to strike a balance between professional distancing and emotional over-involvement.

When Americans ask how to deal with burn-out I suggest a cup of tea and a chat with a colleague at the end of the day. Attending to the needs of others will usually result in the nurse's own 'emotional' needs being met; this leads to satisfaction — not burn-out and decay. Working on a ward with children dying of leukaemia is undoubtedly emotionally draining, but it is these situations in particular which demand a multi-disciplinary team approach, so that each individual is supported by the *whole* team, each of whom will have 'up' and 'down' days.

This apparent digression from the patient's needs to those of the nurse is not irrelevant: the needs are interrelated. If, for example, our attention is on our own thoughts, wants and needs we cannot meet the patient's. This may sound like a sermon, but it is one I preach regularly to myself.

There are no set rules or rigid guidelines to follow in order to help a patient with his worries and anxieties, other than a strong desire to help. If the nurse wants to hide behind a dressing pack in case she is asked an awkward question, that is an indication that the desire is not strong enough. It is not strong enough if she is always too busy to do more than treat the pressure areas and talk of the weather and football results. Nor is it strong enough if she chooses to ignore a tentative, hesitating question from the patient or tells him she cannot answer it when she can. All of these situations occur because the attention is on 'me' and 'my' fears of not being able to cope adequately with the situation.

Only when we attend wholly to the patient, instead of wishing the floor would open and swallow us up, will we understand his needs and be able to respond to them appropriately. This takes practice — for most of us, probably a lifetime. Unless we get our feet wet we will never learn the joy of swimming. As qualified nurses it is no longer necessary or appropriate to seek refuge by passing the buck. If we demand to be treated by others as professionals in our own right, we must be prepared to take decisions, act upon them and accept responsibility for the consequences.

Thus, when a patient says 'I don't seem to be getting any better' or 'I wonder when I'll go back to work', what is the appropriate response? Too frequently, the face cloth is either literally or figuratively quickly applied to stifle further comments. The patient is often told 'Of course you'll be all right, you'll soon be up and about' or 'It's the weather that's getting you down', or some equally unhelpful comment. How often we condemn our patients to walk the road of death alone and isolated: that is not the mark of a caring society.

Dame Cicely Saunders, founder and Medical Director of St Christopher's Hospice in London says:

'Our patients are our teachers'.

Sadly, while we learn, they suffer. I remember visiting a patient who was very weak, who began to question his diagnosis and prognosis. I hesitated, unsure, longing for escape—my bleep suddenly emitted its demanding tone. I had two choices—to remain for a few minutes, ignoring the bleep, and serve the patient or leap up dramatically and dive for the nearest telephone. I did the latter. The conversation was not resumed. The next day the patient was semiconscious—too weak for discussions. I had neglected my patient as surely as if I had ignored a pressure sore. The dying usually do not have time to wait for us to acquire communication skills. The time is *now*: for many, tomorrow will never come.

'But I don't have time to have long soulful conversations', the heartfelt cry is sounded. Again from observation, practice and accumulated wisdom, Dame Cicely tells us:

'Time is a question of depth, not of length.'

With determination and practice comes the ability to turn the attention away from our own ideas of unpreparedness, and on to the patient in order really to hear what he is saying or asking. The time is transformed into depth as the patient is perhaps heard for the first time by anyone.

A West-Indian gentleman said desperately 'What is wrong with me—no-one will tell me?' Briefly, I confirmed his own view about his illness—whereupon his face broke into a smile as he sighed and said 'Now I make arrangements to go back to my family in the West Indies and die there'. No one had actually listened properly to the patient, presuming that although he was asking, he was unable to cope with the so-called death sentence (Aitken-Swan 1959). What had been heard instead were people's own ideas of what, when and whether the patient should be told his diagnosis.

Some conversations will be very brief. If asked about his illness, a patient may reply 'I know my number's up. I've had a good life', and thereafter refer very little to the subject, although he will set about putting his affairs in order.

Mr B. was an angry, determined man, quite convinced that his will could and would cure his cancer. I was equally eager and enthusiastic, having, perhaps unconsciously, challenged myself to help the patient towards acceptance of his condition. One day saw me deeply involved in a wonderful philosophical conversation with him. I left his home glowing and feeling most uplifted. Later, I spoke to the doctor who had visited him after me. The patient's response had been 'Don't let that bl...y nurse near me again'. How I cried when I heard that. It was my own fault; in my enthusiasm to help I had talked at, instead of with, the patient, telling him what I thought would help and what I thought that he should hear. I had not *listened* to him — only to my own ideas and opinions.

We have to listen in order to hear what the patient is saying. However, while learning this skill we can adopt other ways of acquiring the necessary information. 'Am I going to get better?' is a question with a range of different meanings. 'What do you mean by better?' the nurse may parry. Some patients will be asking about a cure for the illness, some whether they will be fit enough to live a relatively normal if limited life, and to others 'better' means the ability to get down the stairs or have their symptoms relieved. 'I know the cancer can't be cured, but can you get rid of the pain?' is the response of some patients when discussing 'getting better'.

Another patient, an elderly lady, who was fading peacefully cocooned in the depths of a very comfortable bed asked 'Everything's all right isn't it?'. A visitor accompanying me began to leap in with an effusive reassurance, but stopped when she saw my face. 'What do you mean — all right?' I asked the patient. She replied that she hoped her relatives and friends would be waiting for her in heaven.

There are ways of conducting a conversation with a patient to encourage him to speak more freely or more precisely. It is vital that such meetings remain fresh and unstereotyped and do not become an exercise in data collection from a piece of human machinery. Every question asked or comment given should be as if for the first time. For the patient it *is* the first time and if the question is put mechanically his reply will not be as helpful as it could have been.

Eye to eye contact can be very unifying, but it can be very disconcerting for the patient to have a nurse intensely studying his face for clues to his reactions. Eye contact should therefore be used with care as it may inhibit some patients from speaking freely. On the other hand our eyes and attention should not wander all round the room and be distracted by trivia. Nobody wants to speak to someone whose gaze is scattered everywhere. A fidgeting nurse can also be a great distraction to the patient; the nurse should aim to sit and be as still as possible physically, thereby encouraging an inner stillness and harmony in the patient.

Giving attention to two things at the same time may mean neither is managed properly. It is difficult to wash a patient well, while concurrently keeping up a non-stop flow of chatter, or attempting to discuss a particular problem. I remember one patient challenging me to tell him about his illness as I was attending to his sacral area. He was quite happy to wait for the discussion until I had finished attending to his nether regions!

It is equally useless to attempt to have a 'meaningful' conversation with a patient if he wants to watch the World Cup finals on the television, or is eagerly anticipating a visit from his grandchildren. If his attention is centred on continuous pain or nausea, or he is longing to pass urine and is too polite to say so, he is unlikely to have a very useful conversation with anyone.

Nature abhors a vacuum in any form. A vacuum of silence may allow a hesitant patient to fill it with some thought or feeling he has difficulty in expressing. However, as with direct eye contact, the silence should not be so extended as to cause the patient discomfort.

It can be difficult to communicate effectively if the patient is sitting on one side of the room and the nurse on the other.

Sitting close together facilitates physical as well as emotional contact with the patient, so that if he is upset and the nurse wishes to take his hand or put an arm around him, this can be done very naturally. We should not be afraid of patients' tears, particularly if it is a man who is crying. The storm will pass and the patient will usually feel better for it. Another way of indicating her willingness to talk is for the nurse to remove her coat before sitting down with the patient.

To assess the situation as accurately as possible, it is usually better to avoid asking a question which demends a 'yes' or 'no' answer. That yes or no will probably be based on what the patient thinks the nurse wants to hear, either in order to please her or because he couldn't hear or understand the question properly. Thus 'How are you feeling today?' will probably produce a more useful reply than 'Are you feeling better today?', or 'What is the pain like now?' instead of 'Is the pain better?'. When washing or turning a patient — 'What is still not comfortable?', rather than 'Are you comfortable now?'.

Asking the questions in this way will allow the conversation to open and flow and enable the patient to lead us where he wishes:

'What was the radiotherapy for?'
'I dunno, they never tell you anything do they?'
'I have your notes here and would be happy to answer any questions you have.'
'The weather's nice today isn't it — it doesn't look as though it will rain.'

In this way, the patient will frequently indicate what he does and does not want to hear about his illness. Some patients never get beyond this stage of denial.

So really it is not a question of who should tell the patient and when or what he should be told (Saunders 1963). He will tell us who, when or what in his own good time: who is whoever the patient asks, when is whenever he asks, and what is whatever he asks (not what we think he is asking).

Sometimes the patient cannot attend properly to the conversation and becomes lost in reminiscences. Repeating a sentence which he has just spoken may help him to reassemble his ideas or realize something about himself.

NEVER lie to a patient. A dying person deserves better than that. If necessary make that quite clear to the family; they may need to be reassured that the patient will not be told anything he is not ready to hear, and that if anyone volunteers information about his diagnosis, it will probably be the patient himself.

If the patient's question is misinterpreted and he is given more information than he is seeking, there is rarely a need to be unduly alarmed. All of us have an amazing facility to interpret or deny what we hear, as we wish; individuals attending a lecture will each remember something different about that lecture. A patient who is force-fed with unwelcome information about his diagnosis from an eager but inexperienced professional, may react initially with despair, shock and depression—while his family seethe furiously in the background. Usually, the patient will have reverted to his former self by the next day, having no apparent memory of the conversation, while the family remain seething and raining curses on the head of the perpetrator of the crime! It is a source of wonderment how thorough the denial process can be. Sometimes a patient will acknowledge that he has cancer, that he probably has not got long to live, BUT 'if only I could eat more, I'd soon be up and about and feeling better'.

Anger may not be acknowledged by the patient until he is asked directly if he feels angry. He will often initially look surprised and then relieved as he realizes and is able to give expression to that anger. 'Why me?' 'It isn't fair', 'I've worked hard all my life', 'Why don't criminals have to suffer?', 'I feel cheated'. Many a patient and spouse does feel cheated and it is particularly sad to meet a couple who have lived their lives anticipating retirement to a dream cottage. When at the age of perhaps 64 years and 9 months the patient dies, the spouse may be totally shattered not only because of the loss of a loved one, but also because of the loss of a life-long dream.

The patient's anger and frustration is often directed towards his nearest and dearest, which may upset him as much as the recipient. Some of this frustration arises from increasing physical weakness and incapacity. Helping the patient to understand this and come to terms with it may reduce a little of his irritation. Occasionally the patient's anger and petty behaviour may need to be checked by some 'straight talking' when it is obvious that his actions are becoming excessively self-centred and that his wife is suffering needlessly. I stress that only a few patients require this approach.

A bargaining approach can be seen in some patients, but it is likely that much of the negotiation takes place between the patient and his spiritual beliefs and is not actually verbalized. From the results, some very good bargains seem to be struck! Mrs B. had a strong religious faith and a large, happy family. With her pain under control and mobility restored, she had come to accept her limited prognosis. Who knows what she offered her Maker, but various birthdays and anniversaries were celebrated. She then fulfilled a great desire by visiting Lourdes in France with her husband. The next event was the wedding of one of her sons. By this time she was very ill. We got her to the church on time—in a wheelchair, with the aid of the St John Ambulance Brigade. Still playing for time, she subsequently announced she wanted to be alive for the birth of yet another grandchild, which was imminent. This request was denied her for she died peacefully, shortly after her son's wedding.

Depression is characterized by lack of interest in things and people. If this includes the patient's family he may feel guilty. He may have difficulty in sleeping properly, and cannot see any point in living. If suicidal thoughts are suspected, the nurse should attempt to confirm her suspicions. Thus if a patient says life is not worth living she can ask if he has ever contemplated doing anything about it. Most patients look surprised and say 'no'. In fact, suicidal attempts appear to have been quite rare, certainly among the several thousand dying patients I have known.

A philosophical digression follows. I believe that suicide, actual or attempted, is comparatively rare, because for most people life is sweet, however distorted we as observers may consider their lives to have become. Although approaching death is acknowledged, it is always hoped to be round the next corner and not this one. Hence, a 95-year-old lady is likely to believe she will reach 96. However old we may be, we all tend to hope that we will beat all the records. Some of our patients initially wanted to die, but after being relieved of their symptoms rapidly realized that that, not death, was what they had really wanted (Saunders 1976). In my view the euthanasia lobby totally underestimates the realities of human nature, and is simply irrelevant. The only use of such a lobby is to illustrate the depths to which society can sink if it does not continue to fight for the virtues of life—hard work, love and self-sacrifice. The nursing profession, above all, must travel the somewhat stony, steep road of loving our neighbour. It was certainly not the thought of unlimited financial reward and an easy life that beckoned us into this profession!

Some patients do achieve an acceptance of their situation. Strong religious convictions are not necessarily a guaranteed passport to a state of bliss. It may be difficult to distinguish between resignation and acceptance: the latter is much more positive and the patient exhibits a quiet, unshakable strength. This can be quite distressing for the family if they have not reached the same stage of acceptance and continue to hope and fight for a miracle.

A patient's attitude will vary according to his current state—angry one day and calm another. Depression may lift as a particular problem is resolved, only to descend again with the onset of another.

However, one attitude usually predominates—an angry, fighting man may die in that state. A person with a tendency to depression may remain relatively resigned and apathetic, and attitudes of denial may fluctuate dramatically—as illustrated by the patient at the beginning of this chapter.

Many of the patient's non-physical problems are centred around fear. He may have considerable difficulty in acknowledging and speaking about them. Instead of 'Cheer up, you'll feel better when the weather improves tomorrow' try 'Mr Smith, you do look frightened/miserable/depressed/anxious' (if he does). Saying something like 'It's hard work being ill, isn't it?', will often produce a voluble reaction from the patient.

If a patient acknowledges fear, the nurse might ask him what he is most afraid of. Pain and suffering are usually high on the list. Much positive reassurance is needed: actions speak louder than words and the patient will soon know if such reassurance can be trusted. Many are afraid of what death itself will be like. I can only offer them my observation of many other patients in a similar situation—that dying is as natural as being born and appears to become easier to contemplate as the time for it draws nearer. The preceding weeks of being divided between clinging to life and accepting death seem to be much more difficult. That kind of information is usually combined with the assurance that he will probably become more sleepy towards the end, although it may be necessary to watch that the patient does not then become afraid to go to sleep in case he might not wake up.

Fear of choking and suffocating to death is a relatively common belief and must be openly discussed. Some patients with carcinoma of the bronchus develop a hoarse voice from recurrent laryngeal nerve palsy. They interpret this as the cancer gradually creeping up their chest to the throat and eventually throttling them — a terrifying prospect from which they must be released.

Sometimes the patient is afraid of what will happen when he is unconscious. He may be distressed and in need of reassurance about disgracing himself in some way, perhaps by incontinence or confusion.

Some patients will resist any form of sedation, tranquilization or analgesia if they believe it will affect their spiritual efforts and cloud their consciousness. If a patient is alert he must be permitted to make such decisions — indeed, the medication should be adjusted if a patient reports any unwelcome reactions to it. How should the situation be viewed if the patient is semi-conscious and restless with pneumonia or cerebral metastases? Can the eternal, unchanging consciousness be affected by the limited physical and mental realms? When a man is unconscious to this world, can his spirit be deflected from seeking the next? Is a distressed, restless body and confused semiconscious mind more likely to seek spiritual union than one which is resting peacefully with some sedation? If we doubt the ancient scriptures concerning the indestructible nature of the Self, there are numerous recent publications which may be more acceptable (see bibliography).

Some patients have a great fear of being buried or cremated while they are still alive and should obviously be reassured about that.

For others, their greatest fear is of being a burden on the family because of weakness and immobility. Asking such patients if they would consider their spouse a burden if the situation was reversed, usually brings some consolation to them with the realization that under those circumstances they would be more than happy to do all they could. The feeling of being a burden also stems from an ability to work. Some patients are roused by being told that they have lots of work to do but that it is very different and probably more difficult than any they have ever done. A look of curious interest will then appear, together with a nod of recognition on being told that the work is to learn to accept, and freely allow others to serve him. For most people this incredibly difficult. Most of us are used to being independent, doing and giving for and to others. Most of us find it difficult to receive. Even a compliment about a dress will often be dismissed with 'Oh, it's only an old rag!'. Being unable to receive makes it very hard for those wanting to give. If a patient can understand that he will help himself and the family, and certainly not be a burden.

Fears about the future of the family may loom large. Many people cannot rest until they have made a will and planned as much as possible—some will even give instructions about the funeral. Many men worry, knowing that their wives have relied on them for maintenance work around the home and looking after the domestic finances. The ladies worry that their husbands will not be able to cook and care for themselves adequately.

Although I have no research-based evidence for it, I have a strong impression that a high proportion of dying mothers who have young children, show an amazing acceptance of imminent death, clouded only by concern for the future welfare of the children. Anxiety about their own condition seems to be displaced by a sadness for their offspring.

When a patient no longer wishes to discuss difficult matters, he will indicate this by a fairly abrupt change of topic of conversation. His lead should be followed. Sometimes a dialogue may go round in circles and this is an indication to the nurse that it is probably time to pursue another topic—or end the meeting for that day. Following an intense conversation about diagnosis or prognosis, the patient's attention should be redirected back to more mundane matters before leaving him.

No doubt his mind will return frequently to the discussion, but it is important to encourage him to live one day at a time.

Many patients will ask if it is all right to hope. Hope is important to a patient's morale, but it should not be used as a shield for the nurse to hide behind, thereby encouraging the patient's denial of the situation.

After he has begun to talk or ask about his condition the aim should be for the patient to share that knowledge with his wife. He may resist, feeling that it would upset her. Or he may become very angry as he realizes that the family has known about his condition for months—hence their strange behaviour towards him. He will be angry with the doctors, also, who have lied to him for so long. Tact and patience are needed to help the patient through this phase so that at last he and his wife can share these troubled times together. This will make all subsequent care easier.

Sharing the fears of a dying person is a privilege to be earned. The patient has no automatic obligation to bare his soul to us. By our actions and deeds as well as words we must show him we are worthy of his trust and confidence. Some more of Gibran's poetry will express this precisely:

'And who are you that men should rend their bosom and unveil their pride, that you may see their worth naked and their pride unabashed?

See first that you yourself deserve to be a giver, and an instrument of giving.

For in truth it is life that gives unto life—while you who deem yourself a giver, are but a witness.'

The Prophet

Chapter 7

Care of the Family

'Hospice care is family care' has become a well-known saying. If practised more widely, it would considerably improve the general health of the nation. When a patient and family are considered as one, preventive care occurs as a natural by-product. For example, the patient's last illness and death will be engraved in the memory of the closest relatives. Their subsequent attitude and approach to life, and their physical, mental and emotional well-being will all be affected by that memory (Earnshaw-Smith 1981). The ripples of one person's life will reverberate through the lives of others—this phenomenon occurs with any human interaction.

The principal role of the professional in caring for relatives is the uprooting of fear. Listed below are the fears most frequently experienced: if these are inadequately resolved, some relatives may suffer from permanent disability. Conversely, resolution of fears will promote peace and harmony in the household—with equally far-reaching effects.

Common Fears

Fear of not knowing what to look for to know that his condition is deteriorating.

Fear of the patient suffering and dying in pain and agony.

Fear of not getting professional help when it is needed.

Fear of being in some way responsible for the illness by not having looked after the patient properly during his life—for example, by not persuading him to stop smoking.

Fear of not being able to care for the patient properly, especially as death approaches.

Fear of hurting him in any way when performing physical care.

Fear of being alone in the house at the moment of death.

Fear of the patient guessing his diagnosis by seeing how upset the spouse is.

Fear of being a nuisance and having to rely on others for help.

Fear of 'falling out' with other members of the family who believe the patient should be in hospital.

Fear of perhaps acting wrongly in wanting the patient to remain at home.

Fear of not recognizing if the patient has died.

Fear of what to do when the patient has died.

Fear of financial problems caused by giving up work and perhaps risking redundancy.

Fear of bringing up a young family alone.

Fear of a future filled with loneliness.

Before these fears can be alleviated they have first to be voiced, but if nurses or doctors are unable to find time to allow this to happen, they are failing in their duty. That does not mean there must be unlimited time available at every visit (and neither the patient nor family should be encouraged in that idea). What usually happens is that on some occasions a prolonged conversation is needed, while on others it is not. In fact, as the patient deteriorates the family may require relatively more attention than he does.

Much 'talking time' is spent on the doorstep when leaving. Unless there has already been a chat in the kitchen, the nurse should always pause on the threshold of the house and offer a comment or be available to answer questions.

The word 'cancer' conjures up for many people a macabre picture of incredible suffering. If the nurse talks of the spread of the disease, this is often interpreted, perhaps subconsciously, as a moving organism creeping stealthily around the body, gradually squeezing the life from it. Some people also need to be reassured that cancer is not contagious.

As a result of old wives' tales, stories of what happened to 'old Jim down the road', ignorance, lack of experience, and an overactive imagination reinforced by the carnage seen on television and cinema screens, many people's conception of death is of a violent, disgusting end. There are fears that the patient will burst open at the moment of death or 'nasty' things will issue forth from various orifices. To explain that at death the sphincters relax and bowel or bladder may empty, or that very occasionally there may be some vomit, and that the patient will *not* choke to death for any reason, usually produces a visible relaxation of an anxious face.

The likely progression of the patient's physical decline must be explained before it occurs so that the spouse will not be so alarmed at the changes she observes. It is also better to present the picture a little at a time—too much information will not be absorbed or understood and can be distorted. The information given will often have to be repeated and restated several times, not least because of the feeling of unreality experienced by many when immersed in such a situation: 'It can't be happening to him, he's always been such a good man, so clean-living'.

Reassurance will be needed to ensure the family understands that because of modern methods of pain and symptom control he will not die in agony. Much more knowledge is now available which was not when another relative died perhaps 30 years earlier. That knowledge combined with the ability to ask for help when necessary, will contribute enormously towards enabling a spouse to believe she can cope.

Two issues in particular will require careful clarification and explanation: these concern the use of steroids if the patient has cerebral secondaries, and giving 'the last injection'.

It is vital that a family should be told that any major response to steroids will be temporary. It can seem like a miracle when a patient who has become hemiplegic and incontinent is dramatically restored within a few days to mobility and continence, combined with a return of lucidity. The family must be warned of some of the side effects of large doses of steroids and that it is impossible to say how long the patient's condition will remain stable. Some patients improve for a few weeks, others for many months. Inevitably, the symptoms reappear and it will probably be necessary to tail off the steroids rapidly and treat any symptoms that arise. It is not fair to the family to let them have false hopes; they should be encouraged to enjoy the improvement and extra time the medication has given, but to understand it is temporary.

While the patient is still well enough to take oral analgesia the family should be warned that injections may become necessary if at some stage he cannot swallow. It should be explained that the injections will probably contain the same dose of analgesia as his oral medication. They will accept it even more easily if told that, because unconscious people can feel pain, it is therefore necessary to continue with pain-relieving medication by injection. If the family is not prepared for this they may believe that the nurse 'finished off' the patient, however many injections he receives or however long after the injection he died.

During the course of the explanation care should be taken not to plant ideas inadvertently into the relatives' minds, or needless distress will result, with the nurse fighting a defensive rearguard action—helpful to no one.

Relatives are often racked by feelings of helplessness and inadequacy, believing that if the patient had been better cared for in the past he would not have become ill. It is necessary to point out that even if a wife feels useless this is not so. The warm, loving atmosphere in the home she has created fulfils a most basic need of the patient, and without it he would be unable to stay there. In addition, she should be assured that she is the best nurse her husband could have or want. Frequent praise and encouragement is necessary and provides a stimulus for further efforts. So often a relative will say 'I don't know where I got the strength from, I never knew I could do it' or agrees in amazement if the nurse says 'I bet you are surprising yourself by your ability to cope'.

Further confidence will be encouraged by instructing the spouse in aspects of nursing care—although with an appreciation of the likely limitations of old age and physical frailty. Often the instruction is as simple as re-positioning the commode next to the bed for easy access. A caring wife will soon learn how to improve her bed-bathing technique, although she may need frequent reminders about bending her knees to prevent back strain. She can learn how to turn the patient, although it is likely assistance will be needed from other family members.

One of the most important things to be taught is the need to perform all actions slowly and deliberately, particularly when turning the patient. Many people, because of feelings of uncertainty and fear of hurting the patient, embark on such manoeuvres with a rushed, panicky approach. It should be stressed that there is no need to hurry, and that each part of the turn should be planned before it is carried out. This is more restful for the patient and reduces the likelihood of fatigue from jerky, unsure and inappropriate movements. Tactfully discourage excessive zeal when plumping up the pillows and smoothing down the bedclothes, all of which adds to the disturbance of the patient.

The more dependent the patient becomes on others, the more likely he is to become bad-tempered, especially with those dearest to him. A spouse can become very upset, if under those circumstances, the patient expresses a preference for the nurse's ministrations. This is another reason why the nurse should teach the relatives as thoroughly as possible. The spouse will also require help from the nurse to come to terms and cope with this dramatic change in the patient's behaviour and personality. Increasing her self-confidence will also eliminate the fear that the patient would get better care if he was in hospital.

A spouse may get a small amount of respite from her vigil if during some of the nurse's visits she is encouraged to relax — perhaps by sitting in another room with the newspaper — knowing that the nurse will attend to all the patient's needs. Such an offer is much appreciated in some situations, although inappropriate in others.

Another great fear is of the patient discovering his diagnosis. Hence, at the first visit, the nurse may be greeted with 'He doesn't know what he's got, you won't tell him will you?'. The false air of jollity which has been maintained over preceding months will have increased considerably the amount of anxiety and strain with which the spouse is coping. The nurse's aim in the coming weeks or months of visiting the home, will be to enable the couple to face together the cloud looming on the horizon. A couple will have shared so much in 30, 40 and more years of marriage: this is probably the biggest thing they need to share and the one they will find most difficult. Often it is the spouse's denial and inability to accept the inevitable which may create the division. She may determinedly believe the patient has no idea of the diagnosis, but accepts that he is not stupid and could well understand the significance of radiotherapy. She should not, and indeed cannot be forced to part with her denials and fears, but gradually it should be possible for the nurse to guide her through these agonizing beliefs. An enormous feeling of weight and burden is lifted from everyone when a husband and wife begin to communicate freely and support each other.

Relatives can either be an enormous help or another source of fear and anxiety. There are unlimited permutations of the attitude and approach to life of the members of a family. Some families, however large, will rely on one or two members to deal with a difficult situation. Others will set no limits on how or what help they will give. Indeed, it is frequently the nurse who is helped and supported by such familes when she falls victim to her own human frailties such as tiredness. In such a caring atmosphere work ceases to be an effort when all are joined harmoniously to serve the needs of a friend or loved one. Each individual is sustained by the efforts of all.

Here too, some guidance from the nurse will be needed. As the patient comes closer to death, there is a reluctance for care-givers to have adequate rest, food and recreation (some wives will not have left the house for weeks). It is useful to suggest that they should organize a rota and take turns to sit with and care for the patient. If the patient hovers at the point of death for days on end, they will realize how practical a rota can be as they rapidly become tired out by sleepless nights or inadequate rest.

Sometimes a spouse becomes exhausted from a steady procession of visiting relatives and friends, all of whom accept her kind offer of tea and sandwiches, while she waits on them and has little herself. People usually respond to gentle chiding when they realize the extra strain they are imposing. It might be desirable to limit the number of visitors if they are not welcome. The wife can always say 'The nurse says he is too ill to see people'.

Grown-up children sometimes need to be informed that Mum could do with a bit more help, but won't ask for fear of being a nuisance and interfering with her children's lives. They are usually grateful for the information, and after mildly berating their mother, will set about helping as much as possible. There may however be genuine difficulties, mostly the result of social changes in recent years. Many women go out to work and cannot afford to lose that income. Children may have moved far away from the parental home, and have young children of their own to take care of. Many homes are not large enough to accommodate extra people, and we no longer live in the large family groups common in previous generations.

Where family members are neglecting their duty to help, their guilty feelings may lead them to put pressure on the main caregiver to have the patient admitted to hospital. The nurse must give every support possible to the care giver in this situation and reassure her that she is doing the right thing (if that is indeed so) in keeping the patient at home.

It is occasionally very difficult to assess whether or not the situation can be maintained and the patient kept at home. The dilemma occurs when the death is imminent but the family feel they can no longer cope. If the nurse can support and encourage them to keep going for just a little longer than they believe they can go, often the outcome is satisfactory and the family are sustained in the bereavement period by the knowledge that they did all they possibly could. Some people cannot and should not be required to continue to cope under some circumstances. Usually the decision is fairly obvious, but occasionally the decision to recommend admission is very difficult. It is well known that a patient who is moved at such a critical time may die very rapidly—perhaps even in the ambulance. Such a caution may persuade a wavering family to hold on for a while longer.

If admission is thought to be necessary, it is better to arrange it before the situation has deteriorated into disarray, and while the patient is still well enough to settle down into new surroundings. Needless distress is caused by a death within 24 hours of admission—precipitating a coroner's inquest and perhaps a post-mortem.

Should admission become necessary, the spouse will probably require much reassurance that she did everything she possibly could, and has no need to feel guilty—sometimes the patient will, in his misery, suggest that the caregiver wants to get rid of him. This is, of course, most distressing after the weeks and months of loving care showered on him. The nurse will require considerable discretion to soothe such a situation, so that excessive feelings of guilt do not prolong the bereavement period.

As the time of death draws closer the nurse's manner of calm confidence should influence and act as an example to the family. Often they will have many questions and will much appreciate the opportunity to ask them and receive honest answers. It is usually best to gather everyone together in the living-room (or kitchen) and, sitting at ease, allow the family to fire their questions. The result is often a marked release of tension and anxiety.

There is one piece of information that should NEVER be given, however tempting—that of the likely time or date of death. Making an estimate which is wrong (as it usually is) will produce considerable disruption in a family, as they plan for a particular day or week. With explanation, relatives will understand the need to take each day, or even each hour, as it comes as, indeed, they have up to that point. There are so many reasons a family will have for wanting to know 'how long?'. Find out what those precise reasons are. It would be far better to try to advise about these individual problems, such as whether or not to cancel or postpone a holiday; this is more practical than playing guessing games. The family may well have suffered already from inaccurate prognoses from the consultant medical staff.

It will usually be necessary to describe what dying is like. Frequently relatives will say 'It's terrible to see him suffer like this' when the patient is peacefully unconscious. In order to prevent an image of suffering remaining for ever, it is helpful to point out that in fact the patient is peaceful, but the onlooker is the one who is suffering. This realization releases much tension.

If the patient has a rattly chest, a simple explanation should be given, that the patient is too weak to cough up the saliva or secretions in his chest, but that if he was aware of that, he would be restless. Describing how the respirations are likely to slow down and stop—with perhaps a few last little intermittent gasps —will give the family some idea of when the death has actually become imminent. They should also be reassured that it is unlikely that they will have any doubts about whether or not the patient has actually died—it will be obvious.

A spouse will often try to convince herself and others that she has accepted the situation and the approaching death. Suggesting to her that she has perhaps accepted it mentally but not emotionally, gives her permission to acknowledge, with relief, that this is indeed so. It relieves her of the burden of behaving in a way she feels is expected of her by society. It may also enable her to have a much-needed cry, having bottled up her feelings in order to present a brave face to the world.

Her remaining fears will mostly relate to the period following the death. Although she will often feel guilty for allowing herself to think of such things, there may well be real difficulties. High on the list are financial problems. Funerals are becoming increasingly expensive and the Death Grant—a pathetic £30—is hopeless inadequate: it has not changed since it was first introduced and the equivalent sum needed today to cover the cost of a funeral would be more than £400.

Other aspects of fear following the patient's death may relate to the spouse's concern for her children—how much they will be affected by the death and whether she will be able to bring them up properly on her own.

For many the main dread is of the loneliness which they see to be their future lot—being unable to contemplate how there could be any further happiness in life without their loved one.

When the death becomes imminent, it may be necessary to tell the spouse that it will be all right if the patient should die when she is not there or when she is asleep. This is to anticipate guilt feelings which will arise if she is not present at the moment of death. The saying 'a watched pot never boils' can be very meaningful—a relative may pop out for five minutes, during which time the patient dies. Ideally, someone should be sitting quietly with the patient at the moment of death, but if it should happen during the night with his wife asleep beside him, she can be reassured that he must have been very peaceful if she did not wake up at that time.

Some families ask what they should do to prepare the body when the patient has died. It is usually best, if possible, to advise them to telephone the nurse after the death, who, if unable to visit, can give some very simple instruction—to straighten the body, remove the bedclothes and turn off heating, etc. The nurse must judge the sort of state the family is in—some are coping and competent, others are terrified of the prospect of touching the body, but would do so if the nurse thinks they should. The latter category should not be expected to do anything which will increase their sorrow.

Chapter 8

Care of Children —
Dying or Bereaved

Grief fills the room up of my absent child,
Lies in his bed, walks up and down with me,
Puts on his pretty looks, repeats his words,
Remembers me of all his gracious parts,
Stuffs out his vacant garments with his form . . .
Shakespeare, *King John III*, iv.

The Dying Child

Difficult though it may be to accept the death of an adult, the intensity of the reaction to a dying child is far greater. The emotions are tossed in all directions — outrage and anger, despair and misery, energetic activity and numbing apathy. Adults are expected to die, adults have had a chance to live, to sin and suffer the consequences — but how can a child be deserving of the same punishment? In fact, the emotional aspects surrounding a dying child can easily detract attention from his needs.

What are his needs? Essentially of course, they are the same as an adult, but a child has some additional needs as well. One aspect stands out clearly as requiring greater effort — that of enabling the majority of children to die at home rather than hospital (Martinsen *et al.* 1978).

No effort should be spared to achieve a home death. In Great Britain, but more particularly in the USA (Martinsen *et al.* 1977), positive steps are being taken to encourage that aim, either by setting up specific home care teams for children, or by appointing to a home care programme a nurse whose main function is to seek out the children who are dying in hospital,

107

arrange for their return home, and to coordinate and participate in their care. Such endeavours are facilitated by a heightened compassionate response of the professional caregivers to the needs of a child. A child who cannot find a comfortable position will be attended to unstintingly until the problem is resolved, whereas a grumpy, obese lady may not draw out the same determination in us.

Much of the care given by the professional is, in fact, aimed at and through the parents (Martinsen 1980), particularly the mother. The parents will often wish to perform as much of the nursing care as possible, although initially they are likely to be apprehensive about their capabilities.

Paul, aged three, had a cerebral tumour. When we met him he was already unconscious and being magnificently cared for by his mother. She bathed him, turned him, attended to his pressure areas and gave medication and fluids via his nasogastric tube. Together with his father and elder brother they were living temporarily with grandparents, whose living-room had become Paul's bedroom. The hospital had been tireless in their care and supervision (Copplestone 1979). They loaned the cot in which Paul was nursed and supplied clean linen as necessary. The family were encouraged to take Paul to the ward whenever they wished. For the last few weeks they were also able to rely on 24-hour domiciliary medical and nursing service, without which home care would have probably been impossible. Changes in medication or advice on nursing care were given as necessary. The frequency of visits varied considerably, according to his symptoms and the state of the family.

One day while I was visiting, it became obvious that the child was about to die. Without hesitation, his mother picked him up and cradled him in her arms as he quietly died. Paul's care was ideal in so many respects. His mother was exceedingly competent under the circumstances. The family's confidence in its ability to cope was enhanced by knowing they could get immediate help from either the hospital or domiciliary staff. Finally, at the moment of death the family were supported and comforted by having a professional with them, even though my role then was minimal.

Some families will decline professional help from the

community. To accept help is an acknowledgement of the child's impending death, which they may be desperately trying to deny. Such denial can create enormous problems in providing adequate care for the child, and for the family as a whole.

The principles of medication for pain and other symptoms are similar to those used for adults (Chapman & Goodall 1980); dosages of drugs are, of course, given according to age or body weight. Distressing symptoms, or anticipation of them, may produce considerable anxiety in the child. If it is not allayed by reassurance and adequate relief of the symptoms, anxiety may need to be treated with anxiolytics. Chlorpromazine (Largactil) in the following dose ranges may be helpful:

> aged under 5 years — 0.5–1 mg/kg body weight
> aged over   5 years — one third of the adult dose.

Injections should be rigorously avoided, unless that is impossible. If strong analgesia is required, a morphine syrup flavoured to the child's specifications should be used. As with adults, it is better to establish treatment with morphine while the child is still relatively fit, than to withhold it until the child is weakened by torment and suffering and the family permanently scarred from watching such a tragedy. Even young children are likely to require surprisingly large morphine doses — often about half the adult requirement. Older children are likely to need the adult dosage. When the child becomes unable to take oral analgesics, the use of morphine suppositories can be particularly helpful. Mothers should be taught to insert them using a little finger instead of the index finger. Morphine suppositories are available in as little as a 5 mg dose and so the whole range necessary for children is prescribable. The manufacturers (Macarthy's) would probably make a smaller dose if requested.

Nausea and vomiting may be treated with prochlorperazine (Stemetil) 5 mg suppositories (paediatric rectal dose). Constipation, as with adults, will be a troublesome side effect of strong analgesics. This may be more of a problem if the child is too young to describe it.

A child's understanding of death will vary according to age and personality. People who work with leukaemic children believe that many of them realize the seriousness of their condition even if it is not openly discussed with them (Vernick & Karon 1965; Spinetta *et al.* 1973). Children are great observers and rapidly become aware of the change of behaviour of parents and relatives as they stop scolding the child when he is naughty or begin to shower him with a profusion of unexpected presents.

As with an adult, it is important to discuss death and dying with a child if he so wishes. In fact children are frequently able to come to terms with the situation better than their parents who may remain distraught. When caring for a child we are even more likely to hide behind the face cloth or medicine chart to avoid 'difficult' conversations. That desire must be overcome as much as possible if we are to be of help.

Cindy was 15 years old, bravely coping with painful bony metastases which were proving difficult to treat. At times she was frightened and clinging and very demanding, at others her strong Christian faith brought her obvious comfort. Before she died she had shared out her treasured possessions with the family, being very definite, for example, that her brother should have her portable television set, and her young sister should have her jewellery.

Nursing care must be carried out with great sensitivity (Gyulay 1976). The feeling of loss of dignity and independence can be intense, particularly in adolescent children. Having to ask for help to the toilet, or to use a bedpan is a humiliating experience to one who was just beginning to establish some autonomy within the household, and perhaps the world outside. It helps to include the child in decision-making about aspects of care, rather than always issuing statements or instructions.

Life should continue as normally as possible—going to school and maintaining recreational interests. As the child becomes weaker a wheelchair may enable him to continue with interesting outings and events. Home tuition can usually be arranged, designed individually for the child's needs and wishes. Children should not be 'smothered' by concern—a child will be a lot happier if he is allowed to participate in some event, even if he is not considered well enough to do so.

Parents will need considerable support and guidance in coping with their own feelings while also caring for their dying child.

Often they will tend to over-indulge the child—finding it impossible to deny him anything—and they may also be unable to admonish him for being naughty. This sort of reaction may encourage the child to be ever more demanding and manipulative of his parents; over-indulgence should, if possible, be gently discouraged.

In contrast to their behaviour to the child, parents may react angrily to the rest of the world, blaming the medical profession for the poor prognosis, and complaining that nursing staff are incompetent. In their anguish they will often be racked by their own guilt feelings, believing that somehow they are responsible for the illness, perhaps through genetic characteristics or failure to care for the child properly in some way.

The whole family needs to be cared for—in the emotional upheaval it is easy to forget grandma, sitting quietly and sorrowfully in a chair in the corner of the room. Sometimes, however, grandparents can increase the stress by criticizing the parents' efforts and regaling them with woeful stories and old wives' tales. It is occasionally necessary to emphasize to the grandparents that for the sake of the child, everyone must 'pull together' and that his parents need to be supported in any decision-making. Harmony may be established by encouraging a mother to let the grandparents help a little more, if she is being over-protective.

Siblings can suffer enormously. Parents should be encouraged to share information with them as appropriate, although naturally they will find it very painful and want to withhold the prognosis for as long as possible. Parents may need to be reminded that siblings also need attention at this time. Children may become more naughty in order to get that attention. School teachers should be informed of the home situation, so that they can watch for emotional disturbance, and make allowances if school work suffers.

When trying to meet all these needs, it is easy for a multitude of professionals to become involved with the family. It is important to co-ordinate effectively the care and visits and exchange of information, otherwise the family may find the nurse, doctor, social worker, school visitor or educational welfare officer, home help and minister all arriving together, closely followed by a deluge of well-meaning but overwhelming aunts, uncles and cousins. To improve co-operation and avoid confusion, it is sometimes helpful to have a case conference, which can also serve to provide the professionals with an outlet for their feelings of inadequacy, anger or frustration in coping or coming to terms with (perhaps) a difficult situation. Without such an outlet, it may be more difficult to continue coping effectively with, for example, a mother who each day sobs her heart out on the nurse's shoulder, so that she can hold some of it back when with her child.

It may be tempting to try to find an answer to the question 'Why *my* child?'. Generally, there is little that one can say. It is vitally important to be as inwardly still as possible in order that the relatives can freely express their feelings and toil towards some acceptance or understanding of their own. Parents in the Western world today do not expect to lose a child, compared with just a few generations ago, when diphtheria, whooping cough, pneumonia and other infectious diseases, took a relentlessly regular toll of children's lives.

The death of a child is likely to have a profound and prolonged effect on the family. A child having to cope with a bereavement may be particularly vulnerable in coping with the future stresses and strains of his life.

The Bereaved Child

The child's reactions will be related to his age and relationship to the deceased. Before the age of about four months, a baby may not be unduly distressed by the loss of its mother, as long as there is a good maternal substitute. Very young children have no concept of temporary or permanent absence. Thus, to a young child a mother's brief absence to the local shop may seem like permanent separation. If the mother has in fact died the child will grieve, but most gradually appear in due course to have overcome and forgotten the event. However, children who experience bereavement at the age of three or four years are considered to be most vulnerable to problems, particularly to depression in adult life (Black 1976). An effective mother-substitute is critical to the child's recovery. By the age of 9 or 10 most children will understand the finality of death and will go through the same grieving processes as an adult. Their understanding may have been enhanced by experiencing the loss of a loved pet, followed by a solemn burial service in the back garden.

Guilt feelings can be particularly strong in children. They may believe that by some misdemeanour they caused the death of the loved one. Some children will then misbehave more in order to earn the punishment they believe they deserve. It is vital that such feelings are discovered, in order that the child does not go through life burdened and emotionally crippled by such beliefs.

Explaining death to a child requires care. Saying that grandma has gone to Jesus may cause a child to hate Jesus for taking her away from him. Similarly, saying that the dead person has gone to sleep for ever, may make a child afraid to sleep in case he does not wake up either. It may help to say that our bodies get worn out and discarded and that, just like the flowers and his pet rabbit, things die. Whatever the explanation, it should be appropriate to the child's needs and understanding.

Children learn by imitation and can be seen to emulate grief reactions also. It can be quite daunting to visit a home where someone has just died, to find numerous adults in a frenzy of weeping and an assortment of children doing likewise. Having only two shoulders, it is then difficult to know to whom they should be offered for crying on! It is interesting to observe the children as they in turn observe their relatives. As the adult sobs begin to subside, the children's sobs begin to ebb also. The British culture tends to adopt a fairly restrained attitude towards grieving. People of other cultures may express grief by extreme, unrestrained screaming and crying.

Whatever the scenario, it is much healthier for the children to be involved in it than to be shooed out of the house, leaving them wondering what is happening or how to react. Throughout any terminal illness and following the death, the children should remain an integral part of the family. They are often able to cope with these situations far better than their parents would believe. Hiding or attempting to hide them from such realities of life, prolongs and promotes the death-denying fears which are rife in our society. Children will regard death as abnormal if irrational behaviour of adults creates that impression. Thus, if a child is prevented from seeing grandma either just before or after she has died, he is likely to grow up with distorted beliefs. He will fear that whatever was happening in her room must be unbelievably terrifying and horrific if he was barred from it.

It is often necessary for the nurse to explain and discuss these attitudes with the parents, as early as possible. Usually one parent is emphatically agreeing and urging you to convince the other regarding the needs of the children. Generally this is not difficult; most parents respond to guidance in these matters and readily see the sense of what is proposed. They are usually prepared to tell a child of an approaching death in the family, but may need a certain amount of encouragement. Of course, they should wait for an appropriate moment, but that moment should come. If further emphasis is needed, the nurse can point out how much worse a sudden unexpected death would be for the child than one for which he had been prepared.

Following the death, the children should be asked, via the parents, if they would like to go upstairs and say goodbye to grandma. A child should never forced to do this and should always hold an adult's hand in the room. Many will go and kiss the loved one goodbye, with an obvious look of solemnity and satisfaction. I recall some children going to fetch their friends so that they, too, could come and have a look—there was an air of total normality in the household. This viewing should obviously take place after the body has been attended to, so that the lasting memory will be peace and serenity.

Children should also be encouraged but not forced to attend the funeral. Again this is a topic on which parents may need positive guidance.

Although many children will recover from bereavement surprisingly quickly, others may not (Black 1978). Apparent indifference to the situation or excessively aggressive behaviour may require skilled counselling help. The general family atmosphere is likely to be an important factor, exacerbating or ameliorating abnormal grief reactions. Existing social problems, or perhaps a difficult marital relationship, are more likely to precipitate greater bereavement problems in the children than a home with a stable emotional foundation.

If a child has lost a parent he may have to cope with other losses and upheavals resulting from the death. The surviving parent may not be able to give sufficient attention to the child. An older child may be fearful of having to take on the mantle of being 'man of the house', particularly when he has his own adolescent problems to cope with. Substitute mother or father figures are needed so that an adolescent boy or girl has a role model, so vital at that stage in life.

As professionals we ideally require many qualities in order to help families in such circumstances. Perhaps most importantly, it is our sense of common humanity which will encourage us to draw near to a painful situation from which we would rather recoil, or to withdraw emotionally far enough to be able to fulfil our duty as totally as we would want to.

Chapter 9

Bereavement in Adults

> I never said goodbye Peg,
> I never got the chance
> It doesn't really matter,
> For you'll stay in my heart.
>   ER (A Patient)

For most of us the weeks, months and years of life pass with a reasonably predictable rhythm and routine, punctuated at intervals by periods of great joy and great sorrow. In most families there will be the joyful times of love, weddings and new babies. There will be an equal proportion of illness and death. It cannot be otherwise. Yet we acknowledge such truths slowly and painfully. Awareness of being a part of the large wheel of life is often difficult to comprehend. Trees and flowers blossom and die, the goldfish in the bowl goes to heaven and a treasured cat or dog uncomplainingly leaves this life when its time has come. It is a shock to realize, as illness and death strike, that we and our loved ones are part of that great cycle of coming and going. Until that point we assume that our place on this planet is secure for ever, as we meander through our daily life.

I often marvel at the incredible composure and calmness of some elderly people whose lives have frequently been punctuated by death of many of their loved ones—perhaps prematurely because of war, suddenly from a road traffic accident or slowly following a prolonged illness. Such people seem to have been strengthened and matured by each blow. They have learned acceptance of death, having played their part on the stage of life with commitment and joy. Shakespeare, apart from reminding us of our entrances and exits, indicated this process of maturation when he said:

'Sweet are the uses of adversity,
Which like the toad, ugly and venemous,
Wears yet a precious jewel in his head.'
As You Like It, II, i.

People often ask me if caring for dying and bereaved people is depressing. There are two reasons why it is not. Firstly, because of the satisfaction of being able to play a part in the relief of suffering of so many. Secondly, because of realizing through my own experiences and through observing others, that there *is* a part for each of us to act out in the great play of life. All I or any of us can do is get on with our parts. I cannot do someone else's grieving, but I can offer such support as I am able.

Grieving is a process of coming to terms with loss. Most people are familiar with loss—a car ruined beyond repair, the theft of treasured belongings, an adolescent losing her first love. Losing a life partner means also forfeiture of companionship, a particular status in the community, a sexual partner and financial or domestic support. The patient coming to the end of his life is also grieving and attempting to come to terms with the loss of his life. The stages of grief can be compared in many ways with the struggles of the patient.

Immediately after a death, many people experience a sense of numbness or denial (Parkes 1975); 'It can't be true!', 'This can't be happening to me!', 'Are you sure he's dead? He looks as though he is still breathing!'. In physical terms it can be compared with sudden injury—the pain from which may not be felt immediately, for example at a time of danger, as in war. This stage may continue for several days. The bereaved person may in fact appear very bright and cheerful and, according to the family, coping magnificently. When relatives say how well someone is coping, warning bells should sound, in case that phase continues for too long. It is necessary for most people to cry at some time during bereavement, usually early on. The nurse should find out tactfully (if she has not witnessed it) whether the bereaved person has cried. Frequently they have held back so much emotion to avoid distressing the patient, that they may be unable to express it after the death. They may need to be given permission to cry now. Some people, particularly men, say that they do their crying alone, and such feelings should, of course, be respected.

When numbness and denial have given way to the reality of the situation there is likely to be a phase of anger and agitation as the real pain of loss is experienced. Intense feelings of guilt may be aroused by the relief that the death has occurred, and the loved one is no longer suffering. The bereaved person may want to review repeatedly the events of the illness, trying to find someone or something to blame it on and at the same time seeking reassurance that he did die peacefully and he didn't suffer. With such doubts over a peaceful death, the torment of a 'bad' death must be almost intolerable. In reliving the events guilt is also expressed by 'I shouldn't have lost my temper with him', 'I didn't look after him enough', 'I wasn't there when he died'. Everywhere they turn in the home there are reminders of the dead person. There is often a sense of his presence, which is usually comforting, sometimes his voice is heard, calling.

There is the sudden emptiness of life which had been previously filled with ceaseless activity in attending to the patient. The constant stream of visitors, once the funeral is over, suddenly becomes a trickle and then stops. Everyone's life goes back to normal, while the bereaved person flounders in a sea of emptiness, where the meaning of life has become very hazy. A period of apathy and depression may follow. There seems no point in cooking for one person, no point in cleaning the house very much, or even getting up in the morning. There also seems little point in being with other people and making them miserable also.

Slowly and painfully acceptance of the situation develops over many months. Interest in life and living is interspersed with periods of sadness. Most people who work with the bereaved agree that it usually takes a year for the major part of the grief to resolve, and that complete recovery is likely to take 2–3 years. Considering the many years a couple will usually live together, and the length of time it takes to build a loving relationship, it is hardly surprising that this process should take so long. Frequently this is not realized by caring, well-meaning friends and relatives. After a few weeks they may begin to tell a bereaved person to 'pull yourself together'. They are likely to weary and become irritated by the bereaved constantly reliving the recent past. They stop phoning and they stop visiting, and hope that the mourner will act 'normally' and 'get over it soon'.

Who should 'counsel' the bereaved? Someone who has never met the family, or met the family but never knew the patient? Should it be someone highly skilled in counselling techniques? Would another bereaved person or member of an organization for the bereaved be more appropriate? Perhaps the question can be partly answered by considering the state of the bereaved person or family. Is the grief 'normal' or 'abnormal'? Normal grief runs a course along the lines already described. It is unlikely that highly skilled counsellors or psychiatrists would need to be deeply involved. Conversely, where there is an abnormal reaction to grief, skilled help is likely to be essential if future problems are to be avoided (Carey 1977). Abnormal grief is exhibited in several ways. There may be a prolongation of feelings of guilt or depression. Some people withhold proper expression of grief, which may reveal itself during a subsequent bereavement with an excessive or inappropriate reaction. If the body has not been viewed after death it may be more difficult for the bereaved person to acknowledge the reality of that death.

Attempting to anticipate which people are likely to suffer from abnormal grief reactions *before* the death may help the situation *after* the death by alerting the nurse to seek advice from someone suitably skilled (Thompson 1977). It may be necessary to search carefully, as not all social workers and psychiatrists have the necessary experience or ability to be really effective in this field. From my experience I believe that a bereaved person will derive considerable comfort from a counsellor, whether or not highly skilled, who had met the patient, however briefly.

There are a number of factors which can predispose towards a particularly difficult bereavement. For example, a relative who is obviously anxious or depressed before the death, or who is intensely denying the situation, may deteriorate even further after the death. This is even more likely if the bereaved person is elderly and has had no children — having perhaps spent fifty years living only for and rarely being separated from her partner. For such a person the death is literally like losing a part of herself.

Extra problems in the bereavement period may occur where children have lost a parent, and households with existing social problems are likely to have them compounded by the death of a close family member.

Helping people to cope with grief is also part of preventive health care. It has been shown that the incidence of illness and death in surviving spouses rises markedly in the first six months following a death. Widowers in one study showed a 40% higher death rate in that period (Parkes et al. 1969), while widows tended to have more long-term problems. Many people complain of physical illness when bereaved. Perhaps some of this arises from having ignored such illness while the patient was alive. More likely it is a reflection of what is happening in the mental and emotional parts of the person.

The majority of people will cope adequately with their grief, but are likely to feel helped and supported by visits from the community staff who cared for the patient.

Visits made to the home, before the funeral, are likely to be relatively brief, perhaps to retrieve loaned equipment in order to allow the family to tidy up the home for the funeral. Some people also want all reminders of the illness removed as quickly as possible. Often, a week or so after the funeral, the bereaved person begins to experience difficulties — having begun to realize what has happened and thus to feel pain.

The most useful, and often most difficult thing the visitor can do at that time is to sit and listen. The bereaved person may regard her both as a professional, to whom she can say so many things she dare not to others, and as a friend who knew and helped to care for the loved one. Usually with little prompting, there will be an outpouring of feeling about recent events, the past, and what the future may bring. There are very likely to be frequent repetitions. A nod or brief word will usually renew the flow if it falters. When, eventually it has subsided a cup of tea will be made and the conversation may then include a contribution from the nurse, usually in the form of reassurance. The bereaved person must be told that what she is experiencing is normal — painful but normal. When a voice is heard or a presence sensed, some people fear they are losing their mind. They are anxious about their strange behaviour—laying the table for two and acting at times as though the dead person were still there. Many people feel ashamed to cry so much—it is particularly alarming to find tears streaming down while they are walking along the street or shopping.

I think it can help a little to explain that the wound of grief is like a physical wound from an operation—that it hurts a lot, that it will heal, but that a period of convalescence is needed in either situation. It is a time to self-indulge somewhat, to do what you like, when you like (within reason!). So often people are urged and expected to 'pull themselves together': generally, this is because onlookers find it too painful to watch grief for a prolonged period.

Well-meaning friends and relatives may urge a newly bereaved person to go away for a holiday or move house. In most cases this is inadvisable. Medication or physical removal from the scene of the grief, will only prolong the grieving process. In fact, most people feel comforted by being at home and wish to stay there. They may well appreciate having a relative to stay with them for a time. A new widow or widower should be gently advised against packing up and moving house too soon after the death—this would be another loss. It is better to wait until life has settled a little when it usually becomes much clearer what should be done.

Some people cannot bear the thought of sleeping in the bed where their loved one died. Redecorating the room, moving the furniture round and perhaps buying a new bed, will usually solve this problem. Occasionally, a wife will be unable to go into the room in which the patient died. This may remain a permanent state in a very few cases—I recall 2 or 3 such instances out of over 1,000 families. Some people feel comforted by placing a pillow next to them in the bed at night.

For many, the most difficult time is in the evening. A man, coming back from work, finds an empty house, while a woman sits in an empty house waiting for a husband, who is never going to return from work. Many elderly ladies are afraid to go out in the evening or to leave their home unguarded, and consequently suffer intense loneliness and isolation.

Some hesitate to discard the clothes and effects of the dead person. Others feel guilty that they haven't the courage or the energy to do it. This is always a particularly traumatic activity, and it is advisable that relatives help in the clearing out process. A bereaved person should not be rushed or forced into this. Usually there will come a time which is right for that person. A decision to keep the effects indefinitely may indicate present or future problems.

Tending and visiting the grave regularly is a great source of comfort to many people. This too may denote problems if an increasing or excessive amount of time is spent at the cemetery.

Bereaved people frequently express anger at well-meaning friends who suggested that they should feel comforted, because although having lost a husband there are still the children. Equally futile and hurtful is to suggest to a mother who has lost a child, that she can have other children, or that at least she still has her other children. It amounts to a denial or betrayal of the existence of the dead person as an individual — even if it was not intended in that way.

While some parents who lose a child find their marriage strengthened by the sharing of such troubles, others find their relationship irreparably weakened, leading to divorce. They have to relearn how to be an ordinary family again, without the constraints of a sick child, which may have been present for months or years. Because of the awkwardness and embarrassment of others, bereaved parents are especially in need of a 'listening ear'. They will want to talk of the child's life, his illness, his personality, his role in the family and many other things. The memory of the child does not diminish. The Society of Compassionate Friends (Appendix 2) is a self-help organization for parents who have lost a child. The support comes from other parents who have been through a similar ordeal. They can give the help and support necessary, when bereaved parents are perhaps worried about their behaviour and reactions, or those of their other children.

The frequency and number of visits necessary will depend on the nurse's assessment at each visit. Some people need to be contacted regularly for a few weeks, others less often. Some may not begin to experience problems until some time has passed.

A suggested pattern is to visit after one month, three months and on the anniversary of the death.

The anniversary is likely to be particularly painful. There is no need to fear stirring up old feelings as the bereaved person will be painfully aware of them. Memories of the previous year come flooding back. Contact at that time is much appreciated. Many hospices in fact send a card on the anniversary of the death saying, for example, 'We are remembering you at this time'. When paying a last visit, it is important to stress that help is available, if ever it should be needed in the future. Referral to a health visitor or geriatric visitor may be appropriate for long-term needs.

During the initial stages bereaved people often derive great comfort from continued contact and association with those who looked after the patient — much voluntary work in hospices is undertaken by such people. Gradually, as they pick up the threads of their life again, they relinquish that contact. Susan acted as our 'Saturday' secretary for a year after the death of her mother. She then obtained a permanent job and set off to live her life anew.

Cruse (p.144) is a national organization formed originally to support widows and their children. Now, however, the trained counsellors also accept the referral of any widower who needs help or support.

Sometimes it is necessary to give people permission to stop grieving, just as it may be necessary to give them permission to start. They may feel that society expects a bereaved person to behave in a particular way and to continue to feel sorrowful, when in fact she is feeling better. Reassurance is needed that this is not an act of unfaithfulness to the memory of the loved one, and that it is all right if she wants to participate in and once more enjoy the activities of life.

Chapter 10

Roles of Professionals and Other Agencies

Metropolitan Anthony hit at the tendency for the doctor to take the patient towards death, for the nurse to take over at the time of death and then for the clergyman to take over beside the coffin. He suggested that they could all work together.

Report of a lecture from Archbishop Anthony Bloom of the Russian Orthodox Church, at a symposium on pain. *Pulse*, 11 December 1976, p. 19.

Flow diagrams are frequently produced to show how the patient is the centre point around which care is organized. He and his family are indeed at the hub of the wheel around which the professionals revolve. However, the spokes of a wheel need also to be properly in place if the revolutions are to be smooth! Many different people may be involved in the care of one patient, each attached to his own organization with its own structure and discipline. Community nurses will often undertake a co-ordinating role similar to that of their ward sister counterparts — that of engaging and liaising with the services of others to ensure that all needs are met.

Communication

The necessity for effective communication cannot be over-emphasized; if haphazard it can jeopardize successful caring. Success depends ultimately on a *desire* to communicate (usually when there is sufficient concern for the patient and regard for working colleagues). Edicts decreeing that communication shall be done and over-reliance on formalized systems, appear at present frequently to be ineffective (Castledine 1982). 'PA's treated and dressing renewed', continue to appear in nursing notes with a depressingly small amount of improvement. In caring for a chronically sick patient day after day for many years, it is possible (and understandable perhaps) that the nurse notes little that is new. However, a dying or acutely ill patient must be observed with great vigilance. The shorter working week nowadays often results in a patient being visited by several different nurses. Unless the notes describe the previous situation, reassessment is impossible. 'PA's treated' says nothing to someone visiting for the first time about whether the sacrum was normal, red or ulcerating.

Communication is not made easier by the use of jargon. My experience is that long words and phrases are concocted to describe a comparatively simple concept, *and then the long words are abbreviated*! American visitors to this country are often struck by the coherence and simplicity of English English; this contrasts markedly with the linguistic acrobatics frequently encountered in the United States of America. In my view the term 'pressure sore' is incomparably more descriptive than decubitus ulcer or decubiti. Meaningful words are for conveying meaning, not for causing confusion, or creating an exclusive slang to make us feel we are in a secret brotherhood.

There is very little information that cannot be written and left in the notes in the patient's home. If, for example, the nurse has discussed with him that he is depressed or anxious, there is no reason to omit that from the notes—he would not be reading anything he did not know about. It is a question of how it is written, rather than what is written. Some reluctance to write adequate notes arises from duplication—if full notes are available in the office why write them twice? In some instances, where a small or limited number of people are visiting the patient, all of whom have access to the notes in the office, there may be no reason to have notes in the house also. The other possibility is for the office notes to become more mobile, accompanying the nurse to the patient, so that they can be written up at the time; this practice would probably ensure that they contained more accurate information, than when written in the office much later, when the memory of the visit has lost its freshness.

Instructions for night nurses (or night sitters) should be clear and precise, incorporating information, for example, about which side the patient was last turned to (in case he rolls back), whether there are particular positions he cannot tolerate, how often he should be turned and whether he should have a complete or partial wash in the morning. Medication and the range and frequency of doses must also be distinctly set out. Information should be available about who is to be contacted if there are problems, and what to do if the patient dies in the night — for example whether to telephone the undertaker, the district night nurses or the doctor.

There are other occasions when note or letter writing is useful. As previously mentioned, an employer may be more helpful and co-operative about granting compassionate leave if he receives a letter from a professional thanking him for being so under-standing under the circumstances. A visit for an out-patient appointment is likely to be more useful and meaningful if the patient brings with him a letter from his nurse. This should contain information about changes in his condition — the development of new symptoms or the possibility of them — and changes in medication made by the general practitioner, who may not have informed the hospital about them. It may be appropriate to mention that the patient is now aware of his diagnosis but has further questions he would like answered. So often patients forget to mention things or ask a burning question, when faced with the doctor. It is worth suggesting to the patient that he should make a list of queries to take also — if they are not included in the nurse's letter. How often a patient visits the hospital and then comes back having forgotten to mention a new pain, or ask if he should continue with his water tablets.

Some patients will question whether it is necessary to keep a hospital apointment which may consist of a long wait and a somewhat cursory meeting with the doctor. Hospitals, to be fair, often give these appointments to prevent the patient feeling abandoned. If a patient is reluctant to attend, it would be best to contact the hospital doctor or general practitioner and cancel or postpone the appointment. The task is completed by ensuring that any transport ordered has also been cancelled. However, if, for example, the patient has been complaining of a new pain, it would probably be better to encourage him to keep the appointment in case he requires further radiotherapy or other treatment for the new pain or symptom.

Specialist Nurses

Only a few years ago a determined doctor or nurse could, in the course of a lifetime's experience, acquire most of the knowledge required for the practice of all aspects of their respective professions. Knowledge is multiplying with astounding rapidity; no doctor or nurse today can claim to be an expert in more than one or two fields or 'ologies'. In fact, today's generalist is also a specialist. It cannot be otherwise.

The advent of specialist nurses in community nursing has provoked reactions ranging from unreserved welcome and acceptance to anger and resentment. There are stoma nurses, community psychiatric nurses, diabetic nurses, renal nurses and nurses who specialize in caring for dying patients—often called Macmillan nurses. For a specialist nurse to please all of her community colleagues all of the time can sometimes be quite a balancing act. The problem can be compared with two women working in one kitchen preparing a large meal. If they do not work together, each contributing what she is best at, the meal is likely to be mediocre, or even a disaster. Of course, not all dying patients will need help from a specialist nurse (who usually has a district nursing or health visiting background in addition to her specialist training). The aim of such a service, whether provided by individual nurses attached to a health district or as part of a separately-organized multi-disciplinary team, is to be complementary, or 'gap-fillers' attempting to meet difficulties and satisfy unmet needs whatever they may be. One of the founders of the National Society for Cancer Relief was Douglas Macmillan. Where the Society is involved in the funding of specialist teams, either partially or totally, the nurses are known as Macmillan nurses.

Specialism should not lead to fragmentation whereby a patient is seen as a collection of parts, rather than a whole. A good hairdresser will arrange someone's hair in accordance with the total appearance of the customer, not just the hair. A shop assistant may be selling shoes, hats or underwear, but she can still serve the whole person. It should be no different for the 'caring' professions. We can learn to assess and recognize a patient's needs even if we are unable to fulfil them all without other assistance.

Dying patients cannot be experimented on in the same way as a patient with, say, a skin rash. For the latter, several different ointments may be tried over a few weeks to relieve the rash. A patient who is anxious, in pain or vomiting needs to be relieved as quickly as possible. Most district nurses will not care for more than about 12 dying patients a year. A nurse specializing in the work may see several hundred in that time, and therefore by numbers alone must be considered to be more experienced and able to offer advice.

An enthusiastic community nurse is generally delighted to be able to obtain expert advice and will forge and seal her own relationship with the patient and family in her own way, without feeling threatened by the looming spectre of the specialist nurse. Then peace and tranquility abound!

The emphasis on nursing research today is accompanied by exhortations that nurses should be familiar with the fruits of that research. No nurse can be up to date with the research in all fields. However, each specialist should certainly be aware and familiar with research related to her subject—probably participating in some of it. A specialist nurse can then be used by her colleagues as a reference book (which talks)—to be dipped into as and when necessary!

General Practitioners

Communication, written or verbal, with the general practitioner should be as frequent or persistent as necessary to achieve the desired results. In common with all groups of people, there is a wide range in the attitude and abilities of doctors. While the majority give a wonderful service to dying patients, some have their own fears and inhibitions related to death and dying, and want little involvement with the patient or his family. It appears very difficult to amend these attitudes and it is usually impossible for nurses to apply any local pressure for even minimal disciplinary intervention. The Department of Health and Social Security has recently issued guidelines (HC(82)13) on the subject and it will be interesting to observe if this changes the situation.

Of course, most general practitioners desire to serve the patient and family to the utmost. Most will probably have fewer than half a dozen patients die of cancer in a year and are therefore willing to allow the family of a dying patient to contact him at any time of the day or night. This ensures continuity of treatment and is infinitely preferable (for dying patients) to the haphazard deputizing system, whereby a doctor is called out at night without adequate documentation, to deal with perhaps a severe cough or chest pain from a carcinoma. Inevitably the assessment and treatment prescribed is likely to be ineffective. A conscientious general practitioner will also play a superb role in supporting and caring for the patient, family (and nurse), determined to ensure a good death. He understands that 'there is nothing more I can do' is *not* true, and recognizes that the patient is helped just by being visited by the doctor. He also realizes that good communication is essential for good care and doesn't always wait for the nurse to communicate with him first.

Dying patients often require frequent changes of medication. If a patient who is housebound is not automatically entitled to free prescriptions by virtue of his age, steps should be taken to ensure that he applies for exemption of payments because of 'a continuing physical disability . . .', otherwise the financial burden may become severe in a home which is perhaps already experiencing financial difficulties because of the illness. The free prescription forms (FP 91) are available from Post Offices if they are not to be had from the doctor's surgery. It is worth remembering that the cost of some medicines, particularly if small amounts only are required, may be less than the prescription charge.

Social Workers

Social workers, either hospital or local authority employees, will vary in their ability to cope with a dying patient and his family. Many will have only infrequently encountered such a situation and may find that their desire to help is frustrated by their limited practical experience. This can be particularly evident when a child is dying. This is not a criticism, but a statement of fact. Indeed, the social work profession is making determined efforts — individually and collectively — to widen its experience and knowledge of the subject, by holding conferences and seminars and forming groups of those who are interested.

The role of the social worker with the patient and family covers two main areas. One aspect is help with the practical day to day problems (although a health visitor or community nurse may undertake this role). A social worker who knows which channels to use to get a telephone installed, a holiday arranged or a housing transfer, all within a short time, is worth her weight in diamonds as well as rubies! Such people can magically arrange complicated transport, solve insoluble financial tangles and produce financial assistance almost by sleight of hand.

The National Society for Cancer Relief may be particularly helpful for those on a low income. The Society may grant a small weekly allowance for buying 'little extras', and may also make larger, lump sum grants for help with telephone installation costs, purchasing bed linen or anything else considered necessary for the patient's comfort.

The social workers' other role is in counselling both before and after the death. Of particular importance is the need at least to begin to consider future arrangements for children who are about to lose a parent. Similarly, an elderly person about to experience living alone for the first time, may be in a vulnerable position. Within the context of teamwork, the social worker's training is most valuable in that it enables a situation to be viewed from angles other than medical/nursing. While a nurse may, for example, consider the patient to be bad-tempered because of some physical problem, the social worker may discover that his behaviour is an attempt to cope with some other emotional problem, which he has so far only half-hinted at. Assuming that social workers will want to hear about some things, and doctors and nurse about others, the patient will often volunteer different information to each professional.

Health Visitors and Geriatric Visitors

The involvement of the health visitor will vary according to the area of the country in which she works, whether or not she is attached to a group practice, and what other professionals are attending to the patient and family. In particular, a health visitor will almost always be visiting where there are children under five years of age who are about to lose a parent. She will probably have known the family for some time and be able to gauge the probable effect of the bereavement on the children and liaise with the school or educational welfare officer. Health visitors in many areas also visit elderly people and may undertake to follow up an elderly bereaved person. Some parts of the country employ geriatric visitors who are aware and attending to the needs of elderly people. They would therefore be able to offer help to a lonely bereaved person.

The Clergy

The role of the clergy can be vital. I recall an instance when the vicar organized a rota of people to sit with a patient who lived alone, in order that he could die at home. Where clergy are welcome, their presence is much appreciated and their visits are anticipated with pleasure. As with other professionals, some ministers will be able to approach a dying patient with a confidence which he shares with the whole family, while others will retreat behind the ceremonial of a communion service and back hastily out of the door when it is completed. Nurses should certainly not assume, in order to avoid the subject themselves, the clergy will discuss death with the patient. It is in any case quite likely that the content of the conversations would be different—the patient expecting the vicar to talk on spiritual aspects of death and dying, and the nurse on more practical aspects of what it will be like when he is dying. Of course, each situation will be different. Frequently, the minister will have known the family over a long period and officiated at weddings and baptisms as well as funerals, earning the trust of the family. With his knowledge of the family he may be able to advise the nurse on family background and possible areas of concern for the present or future.

Physiotherapists

The role of the physiotherapist can be of great psychological as well as practical help to the patient. Active or passive exercises, or massage when he is very weak, will lift the patient's morale and relieve him of the feeling of being 'left to die'. Light chest percussion and a little postural drainage, depending on the patient's condition, may help to clear a congested chest. The knack of producing a comfortable neck collar to support cervical secondaries, may bring much relief. Many districts now have domiciliary physiotherapists available, although not yet in sufficient numbers. Arranging out-patient physiotherapy is usually impractical and too tiring for the patient, unless it is incorporated in a day unit. In a few areas a service is provided privately by a charitable organization.

Occupational Therapists

Home adaptations by an occupational therapist are usually inappropriate on any large scale, because of the relatively short time the patient will make use of them (he may, in fact, die before the adaptations can be made). Stair rails can be useful and would perhaps be an aid to other occupants of the home. Equally useful would be a bath rail if it could be fitted in time.

Home Helps

The home help can relieve a great deal of the strain in a household by attending to some of the domestic needs. Many home helps will do more than strict duty demands. They battle to their clients come rain, snow or bus strikes, knowing the desperate needs of some people. Elderly people, in particular, may have severe problems, perhaps living alone in poor conditions, refusing hospital admission even when seriously ill, stubbornly refusing to leave their familiar domain.

Meals-on-wheels

This service is useful for a limited number of patients, if they are not anorexic. They may need to be supplied to an undomesticated husband who is trying to care for his wife. Kosher meals on wheels are available in some areas for orthodox Jewish patients. Vegetarian meals, which are suitable for Asian patients, may also be available.

Incontinent Laundry

Very rarely is this service appropriate for dying patients, as any incontinence is usually of a limited duration, just prior to death. Long-term urinary incontinence should be dealt with by catheterization. However, a patient who has an unpredictable colostomy, and difficulty in changing it, may soil a lot of bed linen and night clothes and, provided he has enough of each, may be grateful for a laundry service.

Undertakers (Funeral directors)

Although I previously gave little thought to the subject, the last seven years have taught me much about the immense value of the services of the undertaker. His job is exceedingly difficult — treading a fine line between showing concern and care for the newly bereaved, and maintaining a thriving business. Most undertakers seem to manage the two aspects very well. I have found that their response to being woken at 3 am with a request to collect a body often seems to display less reluctance than mine when I was called, perhaps an hour or so earlier, because of a change in the patient's condition! There can be few jobs which contain so much raw, naked sorrow so consistently. With great skill they extract and supply the necessary information to a grieving family in order to arrange the funeral. They present themselves in a calm, effective and efficient manner. The nurse can assist the undertaker by ascertaining whether the patient is to be buried or cremated. It is not always appropriate to ask for that decision before contacting the undertaker, but if it is done very gently the family will at least begin to consider the question.

Not infrequently, these matters will already have been considered and decided, often somewhat guiltily, before the patient's death.

Occasionally, some undertakers mar the image of the profession by preying on the family's exposed emotions and persuading them to have a more expensive funeral than is appropriate or than they can afford. If the nurse knows of such a firm she will be helping the family by suggesting that they should use another.

Voluntary Organisations

Volunteer or semi-volunteer groups are a resource that should not be forgotten. They may give valuable help in 'patient-sitting', allowing a relative to go out. They may be able to arrange an outing for the patient—even if only to the hairdresser around the corner. Some volunteers act as 'good neighbours', by doing some shopping or have a cup of tea and chat with a caregiver who may be tired and lonely. (Some useful addresses will be found in Appendix 2.) I should like to pay tribute here to a group of splendid London taxi-drivers who, regularly each week, gave up an afternoon to transport patients for an afternoon 'out'.

Enabling one patient to die comfortably at home in the midst of his family can therefore involve the skills and knowledge of many different disciplines, each one playing its part to keep the wheel turning. When the patient dies and it stops turning, the whole community shares the sense of harmony which has arisen. This harmony, a natural product of service gracefully given, is a quality lacking in so many aspects of life today, yet given a little encouragement it flourishes readily. As community nurses we recognise that this harmony then carries us along to meet the needs of the next patient, thereby uniting death and life in an endless dance.

References

Aitken-Swan J. & Easson E. (1959) Reactions of cancer patients on being told their diagnosis. *Br Med J*, **i**, 779–783

Black D. (1976) What happens to bereaved children. *Proc Roy Soc Med*, **69**, 841–844

Black D. (1978) The bereaved child. *J Child Psychol Psychiat*, **19**, 287–292

Budd K. (1979) The concept of chronic pain relief. *Health Trends*, **11**, 69–71

Bullingham R. & McQuay H. (1981) Narcotics could be taken sublingually. *Pain Topics*, **4**(4), 4

BMJ Editorial (1980) Opiate peptides, analgesia and the neuro-endocrine system. *Br Med J*, **i**, 741–742

Carey R. (1977) The widowed: a year later. *J Counselling Psychol*, **24**(2), 125–131

Castledine G. (1982) A poor record in writing. *Nursing Mirror*, 2 June, 31

Chapman J. & Goodall J. (1980) Symptom control in ill and dying children. *J Mat Child Hlth*, April, 144–154

Clarke I. (1982) Old drugs for old aches. *Update*, 15 June, 2297–2307

Coplestone J. (1979) A child dies — and ward staff give support in the home. *Nursing Mirror*, 18 January, 20–23

Earnshaw-Smith E. (1981) Dealing with dying patients and their relatives. *Br Med J*, **i**, 1779

Ettinger D. *et al.* (1979) Important clinical pharmacological considerations in the use of methadone in cancer patients. *Cancer Treat Rep*, **63**, 457–459

Ford G. & Pincherle G. (1978) Arrangements for terminal care in the NHS (especially those for cancer patients). *Health Trends*, **10**, 73–76

Glyn C. *et al.* (1976) The diurnal variation in perception of pain. *Proc Roy Soc Med*, **69**, 369–372

Goodwin S. (1982) HV — by appointment only. *Nursing Mirror*, 14 July, 19

Gusterson F. *et al.* (1979) Analgesia in terminal malignant disease. *Br Med J*, **ii**, 47 (letter)

Gyulay J. (1976) Care of the dying child. *Nurs Clin N Am*, **11**(1), 95–107

Hill R. (1981) Endogenous opioids and pain: a review. *Proc Roy Soc Med*, **74**, 448–450

Hoy A. (1977) Terminal pain. *Nursing Mirror*, 10 March, 59–62

Hunt J. *et al.* (1977) Patients with protracted pain: a survey conducted at The London Hospital. *J Med Ethics*, **3**, 61–73

Lamerton R. (1977) Going deeper into care of the dying. *Nursing Mirror*, 3 March, 64–65

Lamerton R. (1978) Opiate delusions. *World Med*, 25 January, 44–45

Lamerton R. (1979) Cancer patients dying at home: the last 24 hours. *Practitioner*, **223**, 813–817

Lancet Editorial (1976) Osteolytic metastases. *Lancet*, **2**, 1063

Lau T. (1981) The hospice at St Francis. *Honolulu Star Bull*, 17 September

Lewis J. & Rance M. (1978) Opioids and the management of pain. *Pharm J*, 28 October, 395–397

Lipman A. (1975) Drug therapy in terminally ill patients. *Am J Hosp Pharm*, **32**, 270–276

Martinsen I. *et al.* (1977) Home care for the child. *Am J Nurs*, **77**, 1815–1817

Martinsen I. *et al.* (1978) Home care of children dying of cancer. *Pediatrics*, **62**, 106–113

Martinsen I. (1980) Dying children at home. *Nursing Times*, **76**, 129–132

Maslack C. (1976) "Burned out". *Human Behav*, **5**, 16–22

Melzack R. & Wall P. (1965) Pain mechanisms: a new theory. *Science*, **150**, 971

Mushin W. *et al.* (1977) Pain relief centres. *On Call*, 17 February, 10

Norton D. (1975) Research and the problem of pressure sores. *Nursing Mirror*, 13 February, 65–67

Parkes C. M. *et al.* (1969) Broken heart: a statistical study of increased mortality among widowers. *Br Med J*, **i**, 740–743

Parkes C. M. (1975) The emotional impact of cancer of ear, nose and throat on patients and their families. *J Laryngol Otol*, **89**, 1271

Rees D. (1971) Personal view. *Br Med J*, **ii**, 164

Robbie D. (1969) General management of intractable pain in advanced carcinoma of the rectum. *Proc Roy Soc Med*, **62**, 1225

Saunders C. M. (1963) The treatment of intractable pain in terminal cancer. *Proc Roy Soc Med*, **56**(3), 191–197

Saunders C. M. (1976) Listening—a key to control of terminal patients' pain. *Nursing Times*, **72**, 796

Saunders C. M. (1981) The hospice: its meaning to patients and their physicians. *Hosp Pract*, June, 93–96

Speck P. (1973) The hospital visitor. *Nursing Times*, **69**, 878–879

Spinetta J. *et al.* (1973) Anxiety in the dying child. *Pediatrics*, **52**(6), 841–845

Swerdlow M. (1978) The value of clinics for the relief of chronic pain. *J Med Ethics*, **4**, 117–118

Tempest S. (1982) Pain control in terminal illness. *Pharm J*, **229**, 555–560

Thompson D. (1977) Thoughts on bereavement. *Nursing Times*, **73**, 1334–1335

Twycross R. G. (1972) How steroids can help terminal cancer patients. *GP*, 18 August, 13

Twycross R. G. (1977) Diamorphine or morphine. *Pain*, **13**(2), 93–104

Twycross R. G. (1978a) The assessment of pain in advanced cancer. *J Med Ethics*, **4**, 112–116

Twycross R. G. (1978b) Pain and analgesics. *Current Med Res Opinions*, **5**(7), 497–505

Twycross R. G. (1978c) Bone pain in advanced cancer. *Topics in Therapeut*, **4**, 94

Twycross R. G. (1979) Effect of cocaine in the Brompton Cocktail. *Adv Pain Res Therapy*, **3**, 927–932

Twycross R. G. (1982) Report on Poor Pain Relief, Third World Congress. *Pain Topics*, **5**(1), 4

Vere D. (1978) Pharmacology of morphine drugs used in terminal care. *Topics in Therapeut*, **4**, 75–83

Vernick J. & Karon M. (1965) Who's afraid of death on a leukaemic ward? *Am J Disturbed Child*, **109**, 393

Wilkes E. (1981) Drugs for the cancer patient. *Geriat Med*, **11**(3), 73–76

Woolley-Hart A. (1979) Slowing down the inevitable. *Nursing Mirror*, 4 October, 36–39

Zorab S. (1978) "It's the normal routine". *World Med*, 28 June, 28

Bibliography

Ainsworth-Smith I. & Speck P. (1982) *Letting Go.* London: SPCK

Autton N. (1978) *Peace at the Last.* London: SPCK

Bond M. (1979) *Pain—Its Nature, Analysis and Treatment.* Edinburgh: Churchill Livingstone

Bonica J. & Ventafridda V. (eds) (1979) *Advances in Pain Research and Therapy.* New York: Raven Press

Burton L. (1974) *Care of the Child Facing Death.* London: Routledge & Kegan Paul

Downie P. (1978) *Cancer Rehabilitation.* London: Faber & Faber

Dyne G. (ed) (1981) *Bereavement Visiting.* London: King Edward's Hospital Fund for London

Ford A. (1972) *The Life Beyond Death.* New York: Berkley Publishing Corp

Furman E. (1974) *A Child's Parent Dies: Studies in Childhood Bereavement.* New Haven, Connecticut: Yale University Press

Gibran K. (1926) *The Prophet.* London: Heinemann

Grollman E. (ed) (1967) *Explaining Death to Children.* Boston, Mass: Beacon Press

Grollman E. (1976) *Talking About Death: A Dialogue Between Parent and Child.* Boston, Mass: Beacon Press

Gyulay J. (1978) *The Dying Child.* New York: McGraw-Hill Book Co

Hannington-Kiff J. (1981) *Pain.* London: Update Publications

Hector W. & Whitfield S. (1982) *Nursing Care for the Dying Patient and the Family.* London: Heinemann Medical

Hinton J. (1967) *Dying.* London: Penguin Books

Illing M. & Donovan B. (1981) *District Nursing.* London: Baillière Tindall

Koff T. (1980) *HOSPICE A Caring Community*. Cambridge, Mass: Winthrop

Kratz C. (ed) (1979) *The Nursing Process*. London: Baillière Tindall

Kubler-Ross E. (1970) *On Death and Dying*. London: Tavistock Publications

Kubler-Ross E. (1974) *Questions and Answers on Death and Dying*. London: Macmillan

Lamerton R. (1980) *Care of the Dying*. Harmondsworth: Penguin Books

Lewis C. S. (1961) *A Grief Observed*. London: Faber & Faber

McCaffery M. (1979) *Nursing Management of the Patient with Pain*. Philadelphia: Lippincott

Martinsen I. (ed) (1976) *Home Care for the Dying Child*. New York: Appleton-Century-Crofts

Melzack R. (1973) *The Puzzle of Pain*. Harmondsworth: Penguin Books

Moody R. (1976) *Life After Life*. London: Corgi Books

Moody R. (1978) *Reflections on Life After Life*. London: Corgi Books

Parkes C. M. (1972) *Bereavement*. London: Tavistock Publications

Pincus L. (1974) *Death and the Family*. New York: Random House, Pantheon Books

Saunders C. (1976) *Care of the Dying*. London: Nursing Times

Saunders C. (ed) (1978) *The Management of Terminal Disease* London: Edward Arnold

Saunders C., Summers D. & Teller N. (eds) (1981) *Hospice: The Living Idea*. London: Edward Arnold

Schniff H. (1979) *The Bereaved Parent*. London: Souvenir Press

Smith C. (1982) *Social Work with the Dying and Bereaved*. London: Macmillan

Speck P. (1978) *Loss and Grief in Medicine*. London: Baillière Tindall

Stoddard S. (1979) *The Hospice Movement*. London: Jonathan Cape

Twycross R. G. (1975) *The Dying Patient*. London: Christian Medical Fellowship

Vere D. (1971) *Voluntary Euthanasia—Is There an Alternative?* London: Christian Medical Fellowship

Vere D. (ed) (1978) *Topics in Therapeutics*. London: Pitman
    Publishing
Wambach H. (1979) *Life Before Life*. London: Bantam Books
Wilkes E. (ed) (1982) *The Dying Patient*. Lancaster: MTP Press
Zorza R. & Zorza V. (1980) *A Way to Die*. London: André
    Deutsch

Appendix 1

Addresses of some Hospices and Similar Organisations

This list is not comprehensive. Further addresses may be obtained from the British Hospice Information Centre, the National Society for Cancer Relief, and the Marie Curie Memorial Foundation.

A number of hospitals have established, or are establishing symptom control/support teams. These include (in the London area): St Thomas's, Kings College, Guy's, University College, Charing Cross and The Royal Free Hospitals.

Roxburge House, Tor-na-Dee Hospital, Milltimber, Aberdeen, Scotland
Mount Edgcumbe Hospice, Porthpean Road, St Austell, Cornwall, PL6 6AB
Dorothy House Foundation, 162 Broomfield Road, Bath, BA2 2AT
Beaconfield (Marie Curie), Kensington Road, Belfast, BT5 6NF
The Hospice of St Francis, 27 Shrublands Road, Berkhamsted, Herts, HP4 3HX
St Mary's Hospice, Raddlebarn Road, Selly Park, Birmingham 29
The Tarner Home, Tilbury Place, Brighton, Sussex, BN2 2GY
Copper Cliff, 74 Redhill Drive, Brighton, Sussex, BN1 5FL
St Peter's Hospice, Tennis Road, Knowle, Bristol, BS4 2HG
Arthur Rank House, Brookfields Hospital, Mill Road, Cambridge
St Ann's Hospice, St Ann's Road North, Heald Green, Cheadle, Cheshire
Macmillan Unit, Christchurch Hospital, Fairmile Road, Christchurch, Dorset, BH23 2JX
Our Lady's Hospice, Mount St Anne's, Harold's Cross, Dublin 6, Eire
St Columba's Hospice, Challenger Lodge, Boswall Road, Edinburgh, EH5 3RW, Scotland
St Margaret's Hospice, East Barn Street, Clydebank, Glasgow, G81 1E, Scotland
St Gemma's Hospice, 329 Harrogate Road, Leeds, LS17 6QD
St Christopher's Hospice, 51–53 Lawrie Park Road, London, SE26 6DZ

142

Ealing Continuing Care Team, Cherrington House, Cherrington Road, London, W7

EdenHall (Marie Curie), 11 Lyndhurst Gardens, London, NW3 5NS

St Joseph's Hospice + Macmillan Service, Mare Street, London, E8 4SA

Trinity Hospice, 29–32 North Side, Clapham Common, London, SW4 0RN

Michael Sobell House, Mount Vernon Hospital, Northwood, Middlesex

The Hospice of Our Lady and St John, Willen, Milton Keynes, Buckinghamshire, MK15 9AB

Cynthia Spencer House, Manfield Hospital, Northampton, NN3 1AD

Priscilla Bacon Lodge, Colman Lodge, Unthank Road, Norwich, NR2 3TU

Sir Michael Sobell House, The Churchill Hospital, Headington, Oxford, OX3 7LJ

St Luke's Nursing Home, Little Common Lane, Off Abbey Lane, Sheffield, S11 9NE

Countess Mountbatten House, Botley Road, West End, Southampton, SO3 3JB

Strathcarron Hospice, Randolph Hill, Fankerton-by-Denby, Stirling, FK6 5HJ, Scotland

Douglas Macmillan Home, Barlaston Road, Blurton, Stoke-on-Trent, ST3 3NZ

Tidcombe Hall (Marie Curie), Tiverton, Devon, EX16 4EJ

Torbay & South Devon Hospice, Rowcroft House, Avenue Road, Torquay

Hospice at Home, Michael Tetley Hall, Sandhurst Road, Tunbridge Wells, Kent, TN2 3JS

St Barnabas' Nursing Home, Columbia Drive, Worthing, Sussex, BN13 2QF

Appendix 2

Other Organizations

British Hospice Information Centre (BHIC)
Will supply appropriate information to an individual or group embarking on or considering the establishment of a hospice programme or similar project.
St Christoper's Hospice, 51–53 Lawrie Park Road, London, SE26 6DZ
Tel: 01-778 9252

CancerLink
A central information resource for cancer patients and their families. One of its aims is to organize local self-help groups.
12 Cressey Road, London, NW3 2LY   Tel: 01-267 8048

Cruse (The National Organization for the Widowed and their Children)
Offer help for newly bereaved people. It organizes courses for those who work with bereaved people.
Cruse House, 126 Sheen Road, Richmond, Surrey, TW9 1UR
Tel: 01-940 4818/9047

Intractable Pain Society (IPS)
Able to supply information concerning the locality of pain clinics. Membership of the society is limited to the medical profession only.
The Secretary, IPS, Bradford Royal Infirmary, Duckworth Lane, Bradford, West Yorks, BD9 6RJ

Marie Curie Memorial Foundation
For information about their residential homes and advice about the availability of night nurses.
28 Belgrave Square, London, SW1X 8QG   Tel: 01–235 3325

National Society for Cancer Relief
Provides financial assistance for some patients who have cancer. Financially supports or helps funding of organizations caring for patients with cancer.
Michael Sobell House, 30 Dorset Square, London, NW1 6QL
Tel: 01-402 8125

144

Society of Compassionate Friends
Voluntary organization to help bereaved parents. It is co-ordinated by
other parents who have also experienced bereavement.
Mrs Hodder, 5 Lower Clifton Hill, Bristol 8   Tel: 0272-292778

Society for Prevention of Asbestosis and Industrial Disease (SPAID)
An organization to assist a family or individual in obtaining financial
compensation for industrial disease, particularly asbestosis.
38 Drapers Road, Enfield, Middlesex   Tel: 01-366 1640

Appendix 3

Some British/American Drug names

Pharmaceutical Name	British Trade Name	American Trade Name
Chlorpromazine	Largactil	Thorazine
Cyclizine	Valoid	Marzine
Danthron 25 mg + Poloxamer '188' 1G	Dorbanex Forte	Peri-colase & Dorbantyl — similar but much less potent
Dexamethasone	Oradexon	Decadron
Dextropropoxyphene + paracetamol	Distalgesic	Darvon Co.
Diamorphine	Heroin	Heroin
Haloperidol	Serenace	Haldol
Methotrimiprazine	Nozinan Veractil	Levoprome
Metoclopramide	Maxolon	Reglan
Oxycodone	Formerly Proladone	Percodan — much less potent than British dose
Pethidine	—	Demerol
Pentazocine	Fortral	Talwen
Prochlorperazine	Stemetil	Compazine

English/American Glossary

For the reader who may not be entirely familiar with English English!

Bath	Tub
Biscuit	Cookie
Budgerigar	Parakeet
Complan	Compleat B
Chemist	Pharmacy/drug store
Curtains	Drapes
District nurse/ Community nurse	Visiting nurse
Doctor	Physician
Garden	Back yard
General practitioner (GP)	Primary care physician (In Britain everyone is registered with a GP who will then refer to a specialist as appropriate)
Health visitor	Public health nurse (similar)
Home help	Home-maker
Notes	Charts
Physiotherapist	Physical therapist
Pressure sore	Decubitus ulcer
Torch	Flashlight
Ward sister	Head nurse

Index

abdominal distention, 42
acceptance
   patient, 84, 93, 94
   spouse, 105
acupressure, 37
acupuncture, 19, 37
addiction, 30
admission, *see* hospital
adrenaline, 63
agonist/antagonist, 28
air rings, 61
Aitken-Swan, J., 88
alcohol, 33, 64
allergy, 13
Alupent expectorant, 45
amputation, 37
anaesthetist, 36, 38
analgesics, 27–34, 40, 41
   causing constipation, 11, 30, 42
   dose levels, xi
   in children, 109
   informing the family, 100
   intramuscular, 78
   suppositories, 78
anger
   in bereavement, 122
   parents, 107
   patient, 6, 7, 91
anniversary, of the death, 123
anorexia 11, 42, 43–44, 54
   see also diet
antacids, 52
antibiotics
   causing diarrhoea, 54

antibiotics *(continued)*
   causing nausea, 48
   fungating lesions, 62
   urinary tract infections, 52
   when to prescribe, 44
antidepressant, 46–47
antiemetics, 28, 32, 34, 48–49
antihistamine, 49
anti-inflammatory medication, 28, 40, 52
apathy, 93, 107, 118
aperients, 42–43, 54
appetite
   see anorexia *and* diet
artificial saliva, 47
ascites, 14, 25, 49, 51, 52–53, 66
aspirin, 18, 27, 29, 40, 48
assessment, 3–15
   environment, 3–4
   family, 4–6, 10
   home, 3
   intuitive, 4
   patient, 6–15, 40
atropine, 46, 78
attention
   of patient, 89
   to patient, 87, 89
auto-hypnosis, 37
anxiety
   in the bereaved, 119
   children, 109
   patient, 4, 6, 7, 13, 25, 46, 48, 50, 85
   spouse, 5

pacemaker, 12
pain
  abdominal, 40
  adjuvant therapy for, 35–38
  assessment of, 21–23
  bone, 40
  from cancer, 24–25
  in children, 109
  indicators, 7
  nerve compression, 41
  non-cancer, causes of, 23–24
  overwhelming, 16
  perception, 25
  physiology, 18–21
  prescribing for, 27
  professional appreciation of, 16–17
  protective, 16
  religion and, 17
  short relief of, 25, 27
  threshold, 25
  when unconscious, 76–77
  see also analgesics and morphine
Palfium, 25
pancreatic enzymes, 54
Pancrex, V., 54
paracentesis, 52–53
paracetamol, 28
paralysis, 12
paraplegia, 41
parents, 108, 109, 110–112
Parkes, C. M., 117, 120
pathological fracture, 24, 37
patient
  frustration, 7
  positioning, 73
  unconscious, 72, 76
pentazocine, 25, 56
peristalsis, 49, 65
'permission'
  to cry, 118
  to stop grieving, 123
perphenazine, 56

pethidine, 25
phenazocine, 28, 29
phenergen, 49
phenobarbitone, 55, 78
phenothiazines, 31, 47, 48
phenylbutazone, 40
phenytoin, 55
phrenic nerve, 53
Physeptone, 29, 45
physical examination, 14
physiotherapy, 45, 46, 132
pillows, 61, 73
plateau phase, 69, 70
pleural effusion, 44, 53
pneumonia, 31, 46, 77
  see also infection
polythene
  draw mackintosh, 75
  occlusion, 63
post-mortem, 81, 103
prayer, 80
prednisolone, 44
prescriptions, see free
pressure areas, 13, 14, 61–62
  sores, 23, 58–59, 125
preventive care, 97, 120
primary health care team, 1, 39
privilege, 71
prochlorperazine, 32, 45, 48, 49, 55, 77, 109
prognosis, 95, 104
Proladone, 29
promazine, 48
promethazine, 49
propantheline (Pro-banthine), 41, 51, 55
prostaglandins, 40
pulse, 69
pyloric sphincter, 49
pyrexia, 7, 74

Questran, 55
quinine bisulphate, 57